This book is dedicated to
John Edward Bailey
1927 - 2002

MOVIE PHOTOS
Alex Bailey

For over twenty five years I have earned a good living from photography. I have never been put off by the chorus of those questioning my photographic ambitions. I've just got on and done it. As a photographer I have travelled the world, met hundreds of fascinating people, and been to some extraordinary places.

The satisfaction gained from seeing my work published cannot be equated in financial worth but rather serves to confirm my own self belief and determination to conquer my insecurities.

Never take no for an answer!

Alex Bailey

Published by imagebarn.

Acknowledgements

This publication would not have been possible if it were not for the time, patience and dedication of my wife Julie. Thank you.

Graphic design and layout
by Ollie Sparshott,
email ollie.s@zoom.co.uk.
Thank you for an excellent job!

A big thank you to Andy Carrol at Cope & Glory.

Thank you Garth Pearce for your valued expert opinion.

Thank you to all those in the industry for their kind help, assistance and generosity in licensing the images used in this publication.

A donation from the sale of each book will be made to The HALO Trust, a charity specialising in the removal of the debris of war.

Printed in Great Britain on paper from sustainable forests using vegetable based inks.

Printed by Frazer Mitchell, email frazer@maxprinting.co.uk.

Please reduce, reuse, recycle and help save our planet.

DIGITAL RAW FILE 250ISO 17MM 1/60 F4 3200K

Light lanterns

© imagebarn - photo: Alex Bailey

Contents

KODAK PORTRA 400ISO **35MM** 1/250 **F5.6**

Jude Law in Enemy at the Gates

This scene was filmed on Steadicam with several hundred extras over very rough ground, which made it impossible for me to shoot during filming, but I recognised the potential, so I asked the 1st AD to arrange a 'take' for me.

Up and Running

Having left school at the age of sixteen, in 1978, it did not take me long to realize that you work for a long time in this life, and you had better do a job that is enjoyable, and rewarding, as well as being able to pay the bills.

To date, the only thing that had captured my imagination was photography.
At the age of twelve, I had attended a photography club, at school. Like so many, I had been inspired by the magic of seeing an image appear from a blank piece of photographic paper in a developer tray, fresh out of that mysterious and intriguing place with its peculiar and vaguely attractive smells, called the darkroom.
This coupled with an interest, that my Father had nurtured in me, for fine art from English painters such as Turner, Constable and Stubbs through to the French Impressionists and neoclassicism, and my own fascination with all things visual, encouraged me to seriously consider pursuing a career in photography.

Being a so-called mature student, at the tender of age 20, I looked around for suitable courses. Not able to afford financially, the luxury of full-time education I decided to find a day release course that allowed employment at the same time as being educated. The obvious choice was a two-year City and Guilds in general photography. I was recommended to a college in Surrey, England called NESCOT, where I was extremely fortunate to land a course tutor called Adrian Davies, the now published author of fine photography related books.

Within six months of starting the course, I had found gainful employment with *The South London Guardian* group of newspapers, as a darkroom technician. It was my responsibility to process and print upwards of twenty rolls of black and white film a day, brought in by the three staff photographers.

At that time, all the photographs in the paper were black and white, although colour imagery was just around the corner with several national newspapers beginning to print colour photographs. *The South London Guardian* newspaper (which was a freebie that relied on advertising for its revenue) was made up of several editions, published once a week.

KODAK TRI-X RATED 250ISO **135MM** 1/250 **F4**

Annette Bening in Richard III

Printed as shot, producing so many stills on a movie does not allow the photographer the luxury of cropping at a later date; this image clearly defines in camera framing.

Jude Law in Enemy at the Gates

Intimate moments like this are a valuable asset to the
stills collection, useful to illustrate 'behind the scenes'
articles and photos that actors always enjoy.

Each paper was sixty plus pages and with, I believe, a legal requirement to have a ratio of 60% editorial to 40% advertising in order to be called a newspaper, resulted in the need for a large quantity of photography each week to help fill the pages.

The assignments were varied from news stories and editorial features to Church fêtes and cheque presentations.

After six months in the darkroom, I was promoted to junior photographer. Armed with an Olympus OM10, kindly bought by my Mother, a few lenses, and a Weston light meter, I embarked on my career as a photographer.

I can think of no better training for a photographer than starting a career in press photography. As a staff photographer the responsibility of producing images that are usable, in the technical sense, and publishable, in the creative sense, day in day out is a real discipline and education. Often pages would be prepared and laid out waiting to go to press, save only for an image from a photo assignment,

which the *South London Guardian* demanded should be interesting and engaging, not just the expected images often seen in other local papers. Therefore, the pressure was always on to produce a winner.

As staff photographers, we were always comparing and competing with our images. This encouraged a creative and productive atmosphere.

Our, so to speak, 'Bible', at the time, was a book written by Harold Evans, the then editor of the *Sunday Times*, called *Pictures on a Page*. This book contained brilliant information on composition and editing for press images. I read it from cover to cover, several times, and knew most of it off by heart.

Whilst I very much enjoyed my time at *The South London Guardian*, I wanted to deepen my knowledge of photography and broaden my repertoire.

Having also successfully completed my City and Guilds course, I decided to move on......

KODAK EPP 250ISO 85MM 1/500 F5.6

I only applied for one job in the *British Journal of Photography*, and got it, working as a photographer for the *General Electric Company* at their Hirst research centre in Wembley, Middlesex, in the photography and audio-visual department. The centre itself was involved in scientific research.

The in-house photographic department provided a service for the graduates and staff and was run by a very forward thinking woman, who operated a system whereby each week the five members of staff rotated jobs. One week you would do photography, which involved working in the studio and on location around the

Sir Nigel Hawthorne in
The Madness of King George

Photos with movement are always tricky,
shoot plenty of frames and make sure the technical
is correct, ensure a fast enough shutter speed.

©Courtesy Samuel Goldwyn Company
Photo: Alex Bailey

Funny Bones

Don't forget the supporting artists.
It is surprising how often images
like this get used.

©Suntrust Films - photo: Alex Bailey

KODAK EPL 400ISO 135MM 1/250 F4
+ POLARIZING FILTER

campus, shooting on medium and large format cameras. The next week you would do colour printing and processing, the next black and white developing and printing, the next audio-visual needs for the centre and one week you floated, helping out where needed. Working at *GEC* was like going back to college. Everyone in the department had been educated to a much higher standard in photography than I had and were very generous with the sharing of their knowledge. They practiced some bizarre photographic techniques, developed for use in science, and photographed some really challenging subjects such as laser beams; the photographic attention to detail was meticulous. It was a right result getting the job at *GEC* as it really did vastly add to my all-round photographic knowledge.

At that time, I regularly went to photography exhibitions preferring to buy the book, rather than seeing the exhibition, giving me time to study the images in detail.

Favourites included Henri Cartier-Bresson, Bill Brandt, Cecil Beaton, Richard Avedon, Herb Ritts, Irving Penn, Don McCullin, Eisenstaedt, Annie Leibovitz and David Bailey.

Cate Blanchett in Elizabeth

Shot just before a take, the gentle diagonals of
the pink material give this image an extra energy.

KODAK EPP 200ISO **300MM** 1/500 **F4**

Timothy Spall from TV series
Auf Wiedersehen, Pet Specials Shoot

An editorial style image shot to the side of the set
in the evening light on a medium format film
camera using a piece of gold polystyrene for fill in.
This photo made several magazine covers.

KODAK EPL 120 MAMIYA RZ 110MM 1/250
F5.6 DAYLIGHT + GOLD POLY FILL

I really did pore over these books, engraving many of the images in my mind. I am quite sure this has helped me with composition (in conjunction with being dragged around numerous Art Galleries and Museums as a kid by my Father) ever since. That is not to say that one should pastiche everyone else's imagery. Every situation you find yourself in is different, only references always help as a starting point, inevitably, one-day, using ones own work as a reference to start from.

After three years at *GEC*, I began to find the work repetitive and decided the time had come to move on again. Armed now with a good photographic knowledge, and six years working in the industry, I opted for the familiar route of going freelance.

I took some cute photos of my niece and printed them as flyers, which I duly distributed outside schools and displayed in local shop windows and had some business cards made up. I decided that from one particular Monday, I was in business as a freelance photographer. It took a couple of weeks to realize that the rest of the world did not know what I was doing and that this was going to be a bit more complicated than I had previously imagined.

I quickly ended up odd jobbing, in order to make ends meet. By chance, a friend of mine was in a relationship with a young woman, called Rebecca, who worked as a publicity assistant on movies. Knowing I was a photographer she called me and asked if I would be interested in working on a film called

KODAK PORTRA 400ISO **HASSELBLAD XPAN 45MM 1/125 F5.6**

The Phantom of the Opera

The cinematic format and panoramic
stills are related.

©Really Useful Films and Scion Films
Phantom Productions Partnership, 2004
Photo: Alex Bailey

Robin Hood Prince of Thieves.
The film was shooting at Shepperton
Film Studios in West London and they
needed someone as an assistant to
the main photographer, David James,
and as a 2nd unit photographer on
the film, for a few days, maybe longer
if required (I guess if they liked me).
It seemed like an interesting offer to
me, even if I had no idea what a 2nd
unit photographer might be required
to do. So absolutely, I should go along
and give it a go. Rebecca offered to
drive so we met at what then seemed

KODAK EPL HASSELBLAD XPAN 105MM 1/500 F8

like a daft time to be going to work, but what I know now is quite normal for the film business. Probably about six in the morning or close to.

The journey from Richmond to Shepperton, some 12 miles, normally took about an hour in the traffic. At that time of the day, interrupted only by a suicidal fox, and the milkman parked in the middle of the road, it took minutes. When we arrived at the studios we entered another world, in stark contrast to the one we had just left, (which had not yet risen from its slumbers), this world was in full flow.

The first thing that struck me was the sheer size of a film studio with its sprawling maze of offices, sound stages, dressing rooms and workshops. Like all decent studios, the world over, Shepperton studios is like a very well equipped self-contained village that operates as the need dictates. Open all day, and night, if required. Catering in many different ways for hundreds, even a thousand or more people, producing movies and quality television. It takes a good week or so

Atonement Dunkirk beach

What other format could have described this part of the scene so well?

to get the layout and there will always be a corner you do not know after years of working in the same studio. *Robin Hood*, was a substantial production that occupied a large proportion of Shepperton's facilities, not least, several floors of offices. After numerous flights of stairs and endless corridors we arrived at the *Robin Hood* publicity office whereupon

I was greeted by Rebecca's boss, Susan d'Arcy the Unit Publicist on the film; a very well respected, and experienced, lady who subsequently was very helpful to me in moving my career along by putting my name forward for other film assignments.

Most studios have what they refer to as a backlot. This is where they build large exterior sets. The backlot at

KODAK PORTRA 160ISO HASSELBLAD XPAN 90MM 1/125 F8

Eric Bana and Orlando Bloom in Troy

Panoramic if used well gives the sense of scale to a production still that is sometimes lost on 35mm.

KODAK PORTRA 800ISO 85MM 1/60 F2.8 3200K

Shepperton, which is several thousand square metres, was being used as the sheriff of Nottingham's castle, mainly built to scale, so it was massive. The day I arrived, they were shooting a market scene involving hundreds of extras who where already fully made-up, dressed and on set. The logistics needed to get large numbers of supporting artists, and animals, on set, is mind blowing. One make-up and one costume person is normally allocated to roughly 10 extras, so if you have 100 extras there

KODAK EPK 50MM **1/60** F5.6

Richard III

are 20 staff with them. Every 30 or so extras are looked after by a crowd person to co-ordinate and direct them; therefore, if you have 1000 extras in a scene you have at least 230 plus staff. Add the shooting and production crew, which can easily be 300 plus, it does not take long to get upwards of a thousand people working on a film in a single day. Epic productions, like *Robin Hood* and *Troy*, can have hundreds of extras and animals on set every day for months.

With so many people to co-ordinate and get on set, the filming day has to start early, so when I walked around the sheriff's castle set at six thirty in the morning, things were well under way.

KODAK PORTRA 160ISO **105MM** 1/320 **F8**

It was very impressive setting foot on a film set for the first time. With so many extras already in costume and 'dirtied down' to look the part, farm animals wandering around, braziers burning, for effect and good reason, as it was Autumn, early morning, and the extras needed the fires to keep warm.

The ground was very muddy and there was a natural mist floating around as

the sun rose. It was bang on! Just how you would have wanted your first visit on a movie set to be. There was even a lack of film paraphernalia, as the first shot they were planning on doing was on a large tracking crane.

The shot would start outside the walls of the castle, creep up and over the wall, to reveal village life going on inside.

Therefore the whole set would be in shot and everything modern must be removed, enabling the movie camera to pan across the entire set.

Later that morning, I was given my first brief, which was to set up a studio, on a sound stage, for David James, to shoot publicity shots to compliment the photographs he was taking on set. The intention was to shoot the actors

in costume, with props that would include at some point, a horse. To be honest it was not too daunting a task as I had been used to doing set-ups on locations around *GEC* and working on medium format with lighting and Polaroids etc anyway. The only thing that was a bit worrying was the scale of it, instead of using three or four lights we were hiring tens of strobe lights. Still never being one to shy away from a challenge, and with David's guidance, I got going setting it all up. The photo shoots went really well, achieving all the additional publicity images required. The two days work, I had been promised, turned into a couple of weeks work (guess they liked me!), this in turn

led to the other part of the brief: doing some on set photography for the 2nd unit who were shooting with key cast members.

There can be several units shooting on a film at any one time. Some may be just a camera operator and a few personnel; others can be a full unit with as many crew as the first or main unit. If it is decided that they are shooting something interesting and of possible benefit photographically, to the publicity machine, which in fairness they quite often are, the decision is made to get another unit photographer to cover the day's film shoot. This is one of the ways novice film photographers can gain experience.

This is what I was required to do, cover the set on the 2nd unit. The reality was I had not a clue what was required, other than a basic idea gained from watching David James on the 1st unit set. On the basis, the pictures were required for publication, which is what I had done for years at *The South London Guardian*, and the subject matter was extremely visual and easily photographic I felt pretty confident. This is often all you need!

Those first few weeks on a film were a brilliant inspiration, considering that at that point I had not been sure what route my photographic career was taking. I knew I had a natural inclination for photographing people. I had worked well as a press photographer. I also had a good understanding of the attributes of light, having been interested in landscape paintings, and had amassed a good general technical knowledge at *GEC*, in a range of photographic disciplines.

By the end of that first film assignment, it all made sense to me. I could see how my skills as a press photographer were very applicable to capturing the defining images from a movie that are so substantially important in the marketing process.

Renée Zellweger
in Bridget Jones's Diary

This shot says single girl
modern story a good generic
photo, a low angle and long
lens enhanced this image.

Left image
Renée Zellweger
in Bridget Jones's Diary

Defining images from contemporary productions
can be elusive, pre-visualizing images from the
script does help; this image was well described
in the script prior to shooting.

I could also see that my experience in the studio was a
valuable asset, enabling me to do the additional publicity
shots that are often required and there was no doubt,
looking around, there was plenty of money in the film
business if you got it right, helpful for paying the bills!

I decided: It was the film business for me!

**Bruce Cook and Rupert Grint
in Thunderpants**

One of several impromptu set-ups on this photo
shoot, we found the abandoned trolley outside the
photo studio, a wide angle lens used close in adds
to the dynamic of the image.

©Photograph from Thunderpants:
courtesy of Pathé
Photo: Alex Bailey

KODAK EPP 100ISO 120 - MAMIYA RZ - 55MM 1/500 F16 STROBE

Breaking in

The challenge now was to get a foothold in what has always been regarded as 'a tough nut to crack'.

It was the early nineties, and the UK was immerging from a sustained economic recession. The then prime minister, Mrs. Thatcher, had embarked on a campaign of breaking the backs of the trade unions, the film industry included. In doing so, what had once been a closed shop and in many ways was impenetrable unless you 'knew someone!' was opening up and opportunities were presenting themselves. In some ways, I guess I had 'known someone' - my first introduction to the film industry had been through a friend of a friend. Not that from there on in it was a done deal.

It may be that I had decided the film industry was for me but like most careers in creative industries, the route to getting established is by no means clear.

There is no guidebook as such, what I have realized over the years, talking to colleagues that have established themselves in creative careers, is that everyone's story is different. The only common denominator is that when presented with opportunities they have all capitalized on them.

When you cross-examine how these 'opportunities' have arisen, one discovers that they have mainly been instigated by an individual making something from nothing. For example, this might mean, thinking of an original project that has subsequently resulted in publication or media exposure, which in turn has lead to a similar paid commission from a client. And so it goes on…*you make your own luck!*

The other major consideration that is so often overlooked, by those wishing to pursue a creative career, is ones business and marketing acumen. I cannot stress enough the importance of being competent in a business sense. No doubt, many brilliantly creative people have failed because of their inability to deal competently with their business affairs. It is desperately

KODAK PORTRA 400ISO RATED @ 600 **135MM** 1/125 **F4**

Ed Harris in Enemy at the Gates

I love a good profile shot, but with low light and a
shallow depth of field, the right plane of sharpness
can be tricky, the backlight really gives this shot
depth and lifts it off the page.

KODAK EPJ320T 640ISO 180MM 1/250 F4 3200K

**Angelina Jolie in Lara Croft:
Tomb Raider**

Framing using props.

Lara Croft: Tomb Raider
©Courtesy of Paramount Pictures
Photo: Alex Bailey

important that novice photographers invest time in dealing with their finances as there is no doubt that a lack of attention in this area can make or break a photographic career. The same can be said of an individual's ability to promote oneself. In a very competitive market place; scrappy poorly presented portfolios with a lackadaisical attitude are destined to fail. I have so often met aspiring photographers whose quality of work was excellent but presentation and attitude were poor. Inevitably, they do not fulfil their desire to follow their chosen career. Equally, I have met individuals who are not necessarily the best image-makers but their determination, presentation, business

**Norman Reedus
Specials Shoot
Octane**

Willing artists help to
make better photos.
The spoon was
Norman's idea.

©Alex Bailey - photo:
Alex Bailey courtesy
Random Harvest

skills, and attitude leads them to become extremely successful photographers.

I had gone in at the deep end having worked, for the first time, in the film biz on a multimillion-dollar movie with 'A' list artists. At that point, I was not fully aware that stills or unit photography existed to such a greater extent in television and lower budget movies.

It would take me another couple of years to really 'break in' to the industry, via this more modest, but extremely rewarding route.

I had been getting some more assisting and 2nd unit photographic assignments, courtesy of the people I had meet on *Robin Hood*, but it amounted to no more than odd days spread out over

Keira Knightley in Atonement

Although filmed as a wide shot, I am always on the lookout for extra shots within a set-up, hence I saw this tight portrait.

©2007 Focus Features - photo: Alex Bailey
Courtesy of Universal Studios Licensing LLLP

DIGITAL RAW FILE 100ISO 185MM 1/500 F4.5 5900K

James McAvoy in Atonement

Animated, uncomplicated and direct
portraits are a prerequisite.

©2007 Focus Features - photo: Alex Bailey
Courtesy of Universal Studios Licensing LLLP

Renée Zellweger in Miss Potter

A tight portrait with good animation
shot during a take, in the blimp.

©Miss Potter Inc. - photo: Alex Bailey

several months. What I needed to give me an edge was an understanding of what was required photographically for film marketing and publicity, preferably from the very people who would use the material.

With the advantage of now mixing, if only occasionally, in the right film circles I heard that *United International Pictures*, a major film distributor, were very busy and needed some temporary help in their London office, dealing with enquiries from the press regarding films they were currently releasing.

I gave them a call and popped in to see the head of UK press. I started work that afternoon. The office I worked in was mainly involved with the sending out of the very images, in the form of press packs, that I as a stills photographer was required to shoot on set. Working for *UIP* gave me the perfect opportunity to study, in detail, and acquire a much more intimate knowledge of what was required for movie marketing and publicity. Distributors, such as *UIP*, work on a number of releases at one time and keep an extensive back catalogue of previous press campaigns. Having access to years of past film releases, and spending time in an environment that was involved directly with film marketing and publicity, gave me a brilliant insight into the complexities and requirements of the movie marketing machine.

The launch of a movie is a multifaceted exercise. The surrounding publicity and marketing campaign is complex and involves many media strands such as television, radio, print and Internet coverage along with promotional tie-ins. One key area is the star-studded

Bijou Phillips Specials Shoot **Octane**

A good magazine composition with clean
space around for text or other inserts.

©Alex Bailey - photo: Alex Bailey
courtesy Random Harvest

KODAK PORTRA MAMIYA RZ 180MM 1/125 **F16** STROBE + DAYLIGHT TUBES

premiere, often followed by a thumping big party, usually attended by the 'talent' from the film along with other celebrities who are invited to create hype around the release. The after film parties are often very lavish affairs, attracting a lot of attention, the whole idea of the exercise! All geared to getting coverage in the media, to help maximize a good opening for the film. Inevitably, the premieres and parties were well attended by photographers, who fell into two categories, the uninvited mass who jockeyed for position outside the premiere and subsequent party venue, and the very

Madeleine Stowe, Norman Reedus, Leo Gregory, Bijou Phillips, Jonathan Rhys Meyers, Mischa Barton
Specials Shoot **Octane**

Great sets and props can really add to a picture.

KODAK EPJ 320T 105MM **1/125** F4

**Donny Osmond in Joseph and the
Amazing Technicolor Dreamcoat**

With the benefit of shooting from right next to
the movie camera this image made a great still
during filming.

select few who were invited inside the party and had unhindered access to the talent and celebrities resulting in much better photo ops.

UIP who organised premiere parties for their films wanted inside photo coverage but seemed to have difficulty, believe it or not, in finding a reliable and capable photographer. Surprise, surprise, I volunteered my services and landed some of the biggest premiere parties in the early nineties, photographing tens if not hundreds of top talent and celebrities, a very useful addition to my portfolio. *UIP* kindly paid me for my night's work and subsequently allowed me to syndicate my photos, altogether financially very rewarding.

Whilst working at *UIP*, a freelance producer called Steve Lanning contacted me. He was working with *Yorkshire Television* who had adopted a policy of making some drama programmes less like TV and more like movies. They wanted to move away from the traditional approach to TV publicity images, which had the reputation of being rather static and contrived and did not always reflect the true emotion and feeling of a production, particularly dramas shot in the new filmic style.

With the benefit of the unions not having such a stronghold on the industry, Steve and the makers of the new style of TV were able to look outside of the standard TV publicity

Brad Pitt in Troy

A strong still that describes the artist in character.

Angelina Jolie in Lara Croft:
Tomb Raider

A quintessential hero shot.

Lara Croft: Tomb Raider
©Courtesy of Paramount Pictures
Photo: Alex Bailey

KODAK EPJ 320T 500ISO
85MM 1/100 **F4**

parameters for a fresher approach. The result of the tight grip the unions had asserted on the film and TV industry was that there were relatively few freelance stills photographers to call on. Hence, why after a few enquiries by Steve, my phone had rung and I was invited to go up to Yorkshire to work on some of their new style dramas.

I virtually lived in Leeds for six months, working for *YTV*. I remember the sense of euphoria when visiting the *YTV* main reception, which displayed images from current productions, most of the display photographs were mine and they were all used poster size or larger.

Collectively now I was beginning to make inroads. I had worked on a number of films and quality TV productions. I had a good knowledge and understanding of the reason for being there, as a photographer for the benefit of the distribution, marketing and publicity machine. I was circulating in the right film, and TV related company and making more and more contacts in the industry.

It had taken some three or four years, but it was coming together I was beginning to break in!

Dame Judi Dench and Bob Hoskins
in Mrs Henderson Presents
Specials Shoot

One shot from a marketing shoot with
poster or teaser art in mind.

©Photograph from Mrs Henderson Presents:
courtesy of Pathé - photo: Alex Bailey

KODAK EPP MAMIYA RZ **110MM** 1/500 **F22** STROBE

Getting the gig

**Movies can often take several years from their inception,
to subsequent production and eventual release.**

The inspiration for a movie can come from a number of different sources.
For example from a book or a play as an adapted screenplay or written
specifically to be made as a movie as an original screenplay.

A movie is developed by individuals, called producers, or a production company,
and sometimes in conjunction with a director. As the idea crystallizes, there are
a number of landmark events along the way.

Firstly agreeing, and securing, most, if not all of the finance to make a movie is an enormous hurdle. It is likely that some of the investment to make the film will have come from a film distributor or major film studio. They may have invested in the film very early on, based on the basic package offered by a producer. This initial package might have included the script with one or several actors and key personnel attached, in particular those with a proven track record with some qualification of this for example box office success or an award like an Oscar® or BAFTA.

Eventually, when the development team is happy that enough factors are securely in place, the decision is made for the movie to go into pre-production. In the likely event, that a director is already attached to the project, a production designer will be commissioned to help set the artistic style of the film. A director of photography (DOP), whose

responsibility it is for the lighting and camera work on the film, will also be contracted, his preference for who makes up his team will be respected. This will include camera operator, focus puller, grips and lighting personnel. Other key players are also selected and employed by the film-makers, in particular assistant directors, hair, make-up and costume designers, sound mixer and others relevant to the specific project such as stunt coordinators and special effects people etc.

Now, on the basis that the film is so called 'green lit', the finance is in place, artists are contracted, key personnel are on-board, locations and studio space secured, and sets as required are built or being built, a provisional date will be set for the film to start shooting, referred to as the commencement of principal photography. This is the most likely point at which enquiries will be made to potential candidates for the assignment of stills photographer,

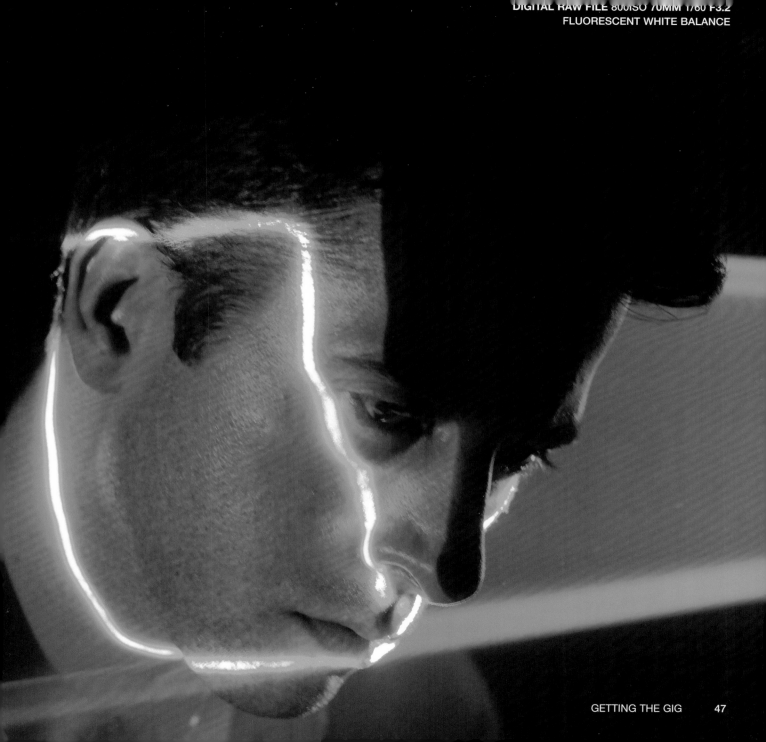

KODAK EPP RATED @ 50ISO X PROCESSED HASSELBLAD X PAN **45MM** 1/250 **F8**

Atonement Dunkirk

A nice moment with the supporting artists between takes, shot on film, which benefited from being cross processed.

©2007 Focus Features - photo: Alex Bailey
Courtesy of Universal Studios Licensing LLLP

probably 6-8 weeks, possibly longer, before the film starts shooting. The first stage of this process, after checking a photographer's availability for a project, will be the submission of a curriculum vitae and portfolio. It is not unusual for up to ten portfolios to be submitted for consideration for a single film assignment.

You live and die by the sword

As a creative person, who produces a very tangible product i.e. a photograph, one can be, and often is, entirely judged on what one presents to potential clients.

It never ceases to amaze me how inappropriate and poorly presented some photographers' and budding photographers' portfolios can be.

A portfolio, whether in a physical form as a traditional hard copy portfolio or in a virtual form on the Internet, is a photographer's shop window. The content, layout, and presentation of that shop window, will have a direct relationship to the volume and quality, of commissions a photographer is likely to receive. When one is considered for a film commission, production

companies and specialist film marketing firms, ask for portfolios from suitable photographers, mostly but not always, from those specializing in the genre. However when the subject matter dictates, for example, a movie that has a strong war theme, portfolios may be invited from reportage style photographers for consideration.

These are put before the film-makers, namely the producers and director, sometimes individual actors are also consulted and their approval sought.

How extensive and varied a portfolio needs to be is certainly open to debate. I can only speak from my own experience, and the success I have enjoyed when my portfolio has been submitted for potential film commissions. Obviously, the physical presentation and the order of a portfolio is a matter of personal choice.

However, in my opinion, the most important section is the one that deals with published material. This offers the greatest reassurance to potential clients of a photographer's ability to produce the images needed to best assist in the marketing and publicity campaign that launches a movie, in what is a very competitive market place. Therefore, images that have been incorporated in posters and brochures and key editorial in magazines and newspapers,

KODAK EPP RATED @ 50ISO X PROCESSED HASSELBLAD X PAN 90MM 1/250 F8

Mischa Barton in Octane

A few set-ups with a single strobe light
in a modern style, ideal for teen mags.

KODAK PORTRA 160ISO **120** MAMIYA RZ
50MM 1/500 **F11** SINGLE PORTABLE STROBE

reproduced and presented as finished pieces of artwork are invaluable. My preference is to have one section of my portfolio dedicated to this area.

In addition to published material, it is important to include work that is considered to provide the raw materials for other uses such as 'making of' books and websites. A portfolio's general appearance should reflect a photographer's professionalism and take account of other factors, such as durability and adaptability. It is important to constantly review ones portfolio and of course keep it up to date with current and relevant projects. I also believe some degree of more avant-garde or abstract imagery should be included, so viewers can appreciate a photographer's individual creativity.

Submitting an appropriate portfolio for potential film commissions is a chicken and egg scenario, in order to get the images that film-makers want to see, qualified by their later use as marketing or published material, a photographer needs to win the commissions in the first place. This is often a slow process, which is only achieved by small steps. In practical terms, this often means volunteering ones service on small or low budget films and local theatre, eventually graduating to TV productions all of which require promotional material, and ultimately into the bigger budget film genre, most likely in the first instance as a 2nd unit or assistant stills photographer.

Once the producer and director, and other interested parties, have viewed the portfolios the favoured photographers are invited in to meet

Jonathan Rhys Meyers in Octane

This was shot after the scene so I could get images direct to camera, it would not have had the same impact if the eyeline was off camera.

©Alex Bailey - photo: Alex Bailey
courtesy Random Harvest

KODAK TRI-X 800ISO 50MM 1/60 F5.6

Luke Griffin in The Disappearance of Finbar

Rising to the challenge of contemporary productions requires some ingenious ideas in order to create images that will stand out when they arrive on a picture editor's desk.

©FilmFour - photo: Alex Bailey

the film-makers. This is an opportunity to discuss, in some detail, how the movie is to be shot creatively, and style wise with regard to particular key areas such as lighting, sets, costume, hair and make-up and any other visual ingredients that are relative. When the film-makers have settled on their preference, and the decision who to hire has been rubber stamped by anyone else with a vested interest, the photographer is hired and terms of his/her engagement agreed. On most decent budget films this will be a full-time contract, for the duration of the movie, which can be anything from six weeks to six months sometimes longer…..

Great work if you can get it!!!

Once the photographer has been contracted, the production will supply them with a script and shooting schedule to read. In addition to learning the story, this also helps the photographer to identify key scenes with good photo opportunities of images relevant to the story of the film and when they are scheduled to be shot. It is sensible at this point to make contact with any individuals involved with the film's publicity and marketing, for example distributors, to get their input and ideas as to what perceived key imagery they are expecting from the film.

Acquiring film assignments is a nerve-racking experience with many contributing factors; undoubtedly, ones portfolio is of primary importance but other factors do figure heavily in the equation not least a film-makers' preference for working with specific personnel, including photographers. It may be that yours was debatably the best portfolio submitted but it does not always guarantee you the job. A bit of luck and a following wind is bound to help!

In my opinion, opportunities can be created (if they do not already exist); it is capitalizing on an opportunity that is the tough part. Someone may introduce you to a new situation but it is entirely up to an individual what develops next and that will be based on one's determination to succeed, coupled with the ability and willingness to improve.

So when asked, as I often am, how I got on in the industry, my answer is

Kristin Scott Thomas in Richard III

Kristin Scott Thomas holding onto her hat on a windy day before a take, an intuitive shot for someone with a press background.

©Richard III Ltd - photo: Alex Bailey

KODAK TRI-X 250ISO **180MM** 1/1000 **F5.6**

"by creating opportunities and capitalizing on them". This has meant maintaining regular contact with existing and potential clients, mainly by email and post, sending up to date CVs and illustrated business cards, backed up by my portfolio, both in hard copy and in a virtual format on the Internet.

Professional presentation, combined with a broad and current range of illustrations of my work, has always been of tantamount importance to me in order to capitalize on the opportunities I have created. I always apply a similar theory when I have secured an assignment. Asking myself before,

during, and after, what I can do to maximize a situation. In the first instance, for the client's benefit, in the form of the range and quality of images I can produce and in the second, for my benefit, with respect to making and developing new contacts with a view to procuring future assignments.

KODAK PORTRA 160ISO **35MM** 1/125 **F11** POLARIZING FILTER

Troy

Production value, images that give a sense
of scale to a movie are very important.

TROY (2004) ©Helena Production Limited.
Licensed By: Warner Bros. Entertainment Inc.
All Rights Reserved. - photo: Alex Bailey

This is best summed up by the phrases: 'going the extra mile' and 'above and beyond the call of duty'. This attitude has always resulted in me achieving excellent results for my clients and being highly recommended, therefore helping to further perpetuate my success in the film industry.

I conclude therefore, that it is mainly ones portfolio that results in one getting the gig, so to speak. By the time one is invited in to meet the film-makers, director and producer, the decision has all but been made. The only possible stumbling block is agreeing the fee a photographer will be paid. Although this is generally pretty straightforward, on the basis the stills photographer will be employed full-time, a weekly salary is agreed for a pre-determined amount of 'on camera' shooting hours, normally a 10, 11 or 12 hour day, with an agreed rate for overtime that is the same as other crew members. On top of that, a weekly box rental is paid for your equipment. If the film is to go on location, then there will also be a living out allowance paid daily. Accommodation and travel expenses are paid for by the production and catering will be provided on location, and sometimes in the studio. If a production only requires a photographer on nominated days then a daily rate is agreed, normally a quarter of your weekly rate.

'One swallow does not make a summer' so continuity of work is important. Keeping your ear to the ground while on one film can often alert you to forthcoming productions that other crew members may have been contacted about. The chance of ongoing employment - send a CV! *If you're not in it, you can't win it.*

Good Luck.

DIGITAL RAW FILE 500ISO 50MM 1/80 F4 5600K

Atonement

I am always on the lookout for shots like this,
a pleasing addition to the collection I never set
this type of shot up, just lookout for it.

Production

In order to have an understanding of how a stills photographer carries out a film assignment, it is important to have an appreciation of the workings of a movie during production.

This chapter is dedicated to giving an overview, in general terms, of an average film, if such a thing exists, although films do usually follow a familiar format.

The production office is the heart of the film; it is from here that the film is organized and planned. It is wise to maintain a good relationship with the extremely busy, hard working, folks that run the production office, provide information, and organize the logistics that the stills photographer, like most of the crew, will rely on.

During the pre-production period the assistant directors, with the help of the production office in conjunction with the director and producers and various others such as actors agents, production designer, location and set construction managers, will compile a shooting schedule. This schedule details all the days a film will shoot for and who, where, and what will be required on each individual shooting day.

Eventually, a start date is decided when 'principal photography' commences i.e. the film starts shooting.

As the chosen day nears more crew involved with the physical shooting of the film are employed, including the stills photographer.

Many of these personnel would have been contracted, or their availability checked and 'pencilled' several weeks or months before. Producers, directors, production offices and most departments are often keen to work with tried, tested and familiar colleagues and those with a proven track record in their chosen field. That is understandable. But this can lead

Joe Wright director and Keira Knightley - Pride and Prejudice

Varied shots of the director are important.

©2005 Focus Features - photo: Alex Bailey
Courtesy of Universal Studios Licensing LLLP

KODAK PORTAL 400ISO 35MM 1/250 F5.6

DIGITAL RAW FILE 500ISO 92MM 1/100 F2.8 5300K

DIGITAL RAW FILE 200ISO **200MM** 1/500 **F3.5** 5900K

Keira Knightley in Atonement

An intuitive shot, if you are not concentrating
and ready to shoot you miss shots like this.

**Joe Wright,
director of Pride and Prejudice**

Shot from a low viewpoint in order to give the
feeling of authority to the subject.

KODAK PORTA 640ISO **85MM** 1/125 **F4**

to a slightly protected environment where the route into any movie-making department does depend on connections to individuals already established in the industry.

The main film unit is made up of the director, assistant directors, continuity, DOP, sound, camera dept., lighting, hair, make-up, costume, props and stand-bys, transport and other specialist departments such as special effects and stunts. Depending on the size of a film and the content of the story, several smaller film units can also be shooting at the same time as the main unit. Referred to as the second or third unit or specific to their task, such as model, stunt, aerial or computer generated image unit.

The making or shooting of a movie is physically grueling. Films often shoot a twelve hour plus day, often six days a week for at least 10-12 weeks and anything up to six months or more. Films can involve night shooting and require the crew to travel to distant and remote places making contact with home difficult.

Relatively speaking being able to conduct a near normal life whilst working on a film is almost impossible.

On a daily basis during the shooting period, a call sheet is issued at the end of the day, itemizing the following day's requirements, scenes to be filmed and the times cast and crew are called to the set. In addition the call sheet provides information on what will facilitate filming such as hair, make-up, costume, and any specialist equipment like wind machines or camera cranes.

Call sheets and schedules are very important and are read carefully by all crew members.

With so much financially at stake, and always so much to organize, efficiency and the sharing of information is intrinsic to the success of shooting a movie. The only thing that can chuck a spanner in the works for movies on location is the weather. But in the event, most productions are able to react with a contingency plan namely 'weather cover' which is an alternative shooting day not affected by weather conditions, usually an interior scene.

During production 'rushes' are viewed daily by the director and key personnel for reassurance of the quality of the previous days filming, resulting in the producer giving the go-ahead to strike used sets freeing up expensive sound stages.

All being well the shooting period concludes, more or less on schedule, whereupon the film production winds down, crew contracts are terminated, sets are broken down, props and costumes returned to hire companies or stored in the anticipation that there may be the need for some re-shooting or a sequel?

The film then goes into post-production. This is when the director starts editing the movie, although an editing department is usually involved during production checking the film footage will cut together.

DIGITAL RAW FILE 250ISO **35MM** 1/160 **F5.6** 5500K

Atonement

Not the most interesting point in this scene for
stills but I always remind myself there is a photo.
Framing in the camera, which was on a crane,
made an intriguing image.

Probably a couple of years after the nucleus of the idea to shoot a particular film was conceived, the finished movie is delivered to the distributors/sales agents in order for the film-makers to fulfil their contractual obligations. Included in this is the material produced by the stills photographer, which will form the basis of the print marketing and publicity campaign. Although it is very likely with a film where distributors are already involved that they would have received material, produced by the stills photographer, during production, as these images are so substantially important in formulating their marketing campaign.

In all, the shooting of a movie is an enormous task, riddled with the potential for no end of problems. Ultimately, it is thanks to the producers and the staff in the production office that movies ever get made.

The inspiration is down to those with a vision and the graft is down to the crew...

Atonement
Keira Knightley and crew

Reportage - one can only capture images like this if you are anticipating them. Preferably with the camera to your eye ready to shoot.

DIGITAL RAW FILE 200ISO 17MM 1/250 F10 5300K

Angelina Jolie as Lara Croft: Tomb Raider

Lara Croft: Tomb Raider
©Courtesy of Paramount Pictures
Photo: Alex Bailey

KODAK EPP 120 MAMIYA RZ 110MM
1/500 **F16** STROBE

UNIT PUBLICIST

Unit Publicist

The film's unit publicist is in charge of anything publishable, printable or for broadcast.

The stills photographer and unit publicist together form the publicity department, and sometimes benefit from a publicity assistant to help with their day-to-day duties and paperwork.   If the volume of photographic work dictates the need for an assistant stills person they too will be based in the publicity office.

The job description of a unit publicist is broad, but typically includes:

1. Dealing with the numerous requests made by newspapers, magazines and TV productions to interview the key players and report from the set. (The unit publicist subsequently accompanies those that are approved, and invited, to the film set).

2. The writing of a film's press releases and the production notes

3. Overseeing the electronic press kit, also known as the 'making of' film

4. Liaising and dealing with requests from outside marketing or merchandising departments such as helping to organize a specials shot

5. Logistics relating to the organization of artist approvals

6. Captioning the stills

Due to the nature of the unit publicist's job, they tend to spend the greater proportion of their time in the publicity office or around the production end of a film. Visiting the set for various reasons but in particular to gain clearance, from the director and the 1st assistant director for set visits from the EPK crew and visiting journalists. Those clearances will be followed up by a memo to all relevant cast and crew reminding them of pending visits and their involvement.

The relationship between publicist and photographer is a close one. On the basis that a stills photographer spends the majority of their time on set and the unit publicist spends theirs mainly behind the scenes huge benefits can be gained by helping and supporting each other. For example, the stills photographer can easily assist the unit publicist with matters set related, due to their close relationship with the shooting crew and vice versa the unit publicist helping the stills photographer with matters production or office related a truly symbiotic relationship.

The unit publicist is generally contracted full-time, the same as the stills photographer. Sometimes the producers employ a PR company, usually if they are to handle the publicity through production to theatrical release. The PR company will then dedicate a publicist to the project rather than the producers hiring a unit publicist directly.

The publicity office sets up a week, or two, before a production starts shooting and winds down a week or so after filming wraps.

Chris Evans in Sunshine

One of the hundreds of images shot during a specials shoot for Sunshine of the actors in a range of sizes, angles and lighting set-ups, all potential ingredients for the marketing mix.

HASSELBLAD HD DIGITAL
100ISO **100MM** 1/500 **F11**

KODAK EPP MAMIYA RZ 110MM 1/250 F16

The Descent

Shoot plenty on group shots, and have the subject move around in the frame, change lenses and your position in order to get a range of poses, expressions and angles to choose from.

©Celador Films - photo: Alex Bailey

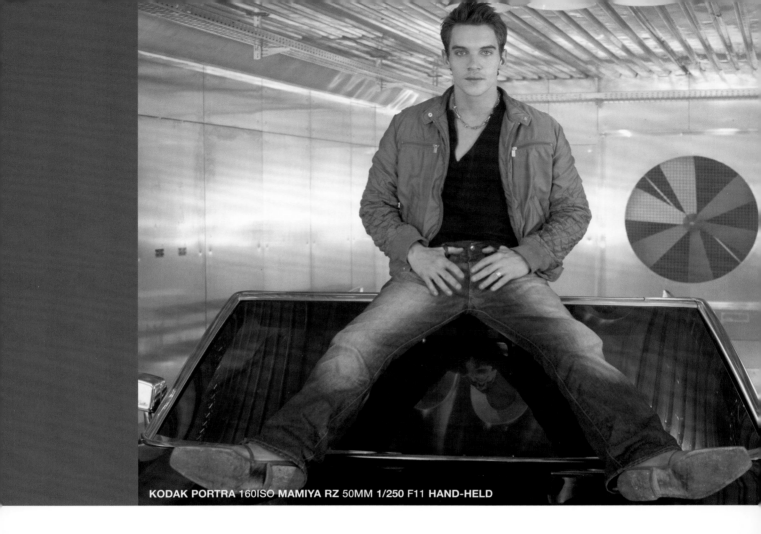

KODAK PORTRA 160ISO **MAMIYA RZ** 50MM 1/250 F11 **HAND-HELD**

All the photographic material, production notes and making of footage are handed over to the production or delivered direct to the distributors when the publicity office closes.

A point worth clarifying:

Publicity is media coverage, print, TV or radio that is generated not paid for.

Advertising is paid for space.

A marketing campaign is made up of publicity, advertising and other promotional activity.

Jonathan Rhys Meyers in Octane
Specials Shoot

An intriguing set and provocative pose makes for a great magazine photo.

DIGITAL RAW FILE 1600ISO 300MM 1/80 F2.5 4500K

The Brief

A definitive still describes a film's emotion in a single image.

When one reads a film script quintessential stills often suggest themselves. It is true to say, that these pre-conceived images often do come to fruition and deliver photos that contribute to what will later be the main selection of stills that represent a movie.

Keira Knightley in Atonement

An evocative image from a night shoot.

©2007 Focus Features - photo: Alex Bailey
Courtesy of Universal Studios Licensing LLLP

KODAK PORTRA 800ISO 85MM 1/80 F4 3200K

**Emmy Rossum and Gerard Butler
in The Phantom of the Opera**

The greatest attribute of a stills photographer
is the instant recognition of a defining moment.

©Really Useful Films and Scion Films
Phantom Productions Partnership, 2004
Photo: Alex Bailey

It is also true to say that often the very best shots come from the most unexpected scenes and moments in a film. This is the fundamental reason why a photographer is contracted for the entire shooting period of a film so they can be there all the time, never missing a photo op!

On the surface, it may seem an extravagance to have a photographer on a film set full-time.

However, put into context with the volume of photography required, and set against the fact that often the marketing spend, when releasing a movie, can be as much as a film costs to produce, the photographer's fee and related expenses are a drop in the ocean. One should also consider what is at stake with regard to the importance of having the range and quality of images required to launch a successful marketing campaign, hopefully, assisting in the commercial success of a movie.

KODAK PORTA 400ISO 200MM 1/1000 F4

Key reasons for a stills photographer's permanence on a movie are:

1. The quality, quantity, complexity and range of images required to represent a movie in stills.

2. Continuity with the cast and crew and the working relationships developed, therefore making it desirable to have the same stills photographer throughout.

3. Schedule changes, due to the very nature of filming, (dependency on the weather for example) the shooting schedule often changes.

Therefore the production office booking isolated dates with a photographer several weeks or months in advance is destined for problems as these dates are likely to change.

Who decides how many images and what of?

Somewhere amongst the many pages that make up the official contract between the film-makers, the producers, and the distributors/sales agents, there is a contractual delivery requirement for specific publicity materials, which the stills form part of.

This reads something along the lines that the producers will deliver a predetermined quantity of still images, of a professional standard, representing the film approved by those contained within, namely the actors (crew members have a standard clause in their employment contracts allowing their likeness to be used in various media formats).

KODAK PORTA 320ISO 50MM 1/125 F6

Brenda Blethyn, Rosamund Pike, Talulah Riley, Carey Mulligan, Keira Knightley and Jena Malone in Pride and Prejudice

Golden moments, great actors, great costumes, great photo opportunities.

©2005 Focus Features - photo: Alex Bailey
Courtesy of Universal Studios Licensing LLLP

Most film distributors and TV companies have published guidelines as to what these images should be, typically:

1. The principal actors in character, in a range of shot sizes and in combinations with other actors

2. A descriptive image from each scene.

3. All the key film-makers and heads of departments

4. Images of the sets and locations

5. Photographs of the film-making in progress - reportage images

6. Key costumes and props

7. Artwork and models

Although quality not quantity is of the upper most importance, the fulfilling of the delivery requirements will still necessitate the taking of several thousand images.

The most important images are those of the actors in context with the set, in a range of sizes and styles. You can never have enough shots especially when you consider that most principal actors will have stills approval and it would be fundamentally flawed to assume one could judge which images will appeal to an individual actor.

Stills approval is either carried out by the artist themselves during production, physically looking at all the images they are in usually on an enlarged contact sheet and killing by means of a pen strike the ones they disapprove of, or by their own personal publicist again marking out killed shots.

DIGITAL RAW FILE 200ISO **135MM** 1/320 **F5** 5900K

James McAvoy in Atonement
Poster art from on set photography

I heard the 2nd unit were going off for the day to shoot James McAvoy in a poppy field; I weighed up the odds with what the 1st unit were shooting and headed off to join the 2nd unit. It's a good job I did!

There is usually a permitted limit to the number of kills an actor can make, with an opportunity of re-presenting a proportion of killed images if required, seldom is that limit reached.

From my experience, there is no rhyme or reason between what is killed and what is approved. How actors see themselves is an extremely personal issue.

Generally, most actors prefer to be seen in stills animated and appropriate to their character.

The unit publicist carries out the logistics and organization of the approvals process, during production.

Artists are equally likely to draw attention to images that meet with their particular approval by highlighting these on the contact sheets.

A few gratis prints of these shots given to the actor can help to foster a pleasant working relationship. Likewise, a few pictures for the crew are always well received and can help carry favour and goodwill, given out on the understanding that they are strictly for personal use only and not for any kind of publication.

Most production photography, from a film, is embargoed until time of release when its use will be controlled and influenced, by the distributors and their marketing departments, with the exception sometimes of an early release picture, mainly for the film trade papers.

This may serve to generate interest in a project that has not yet secured distribution rights in all territories, or as a point of interest to those in the industry as film trade publications often carry a list of the crew employed on a particular production in addition to an image. National newspapers and magazines often pick up these early release photos,

but rarely, at this point do they form any part of a deliberate marketing and publicity campaign.

Broadly speaking the content of stills is down to the interpretation of the stills photographer. This is not to say that there is not a basic requirement. The images, of course, should be

technically correct and professionally composed. If the stills photographer did nothing else other than stand next to the movie camera throughout, and replicate what it shoots, this alone would provide the contractual requirements by definition because most scenes are shot wide, close and in various lens sizes and angles on the actors.

DIGITAL RAW FILE 400ISO **300MM** 1/500 **F6.3** 5500K

Keira Knightley in Atonement
Poster art from on set photography

It was just ideal, the summer Atonement was shot,
it was hot and sweltering at times, it exactly
reflected the atmosphere in the book.

KODAK PORTRA 160ISO 105MM 1/250 F10

The History Boys in The History Boys
- additional set photography

I really put my mind to thinking of as many
group shots as I could when I was on set
for The 'History Boys'.

**Writer Alan Bennett
and director
Nicholas Hytner
on the set of
The History Boys.**

A really important photo for this
film, where the writer and director
are well known. Individual shots
were important, as were two
shots as their collaboration had
a successful proven track record.

©History Boys Ltd
Photo: Alex Bailey
By kind permission of Nicholas
Hytner and Alan Bennett

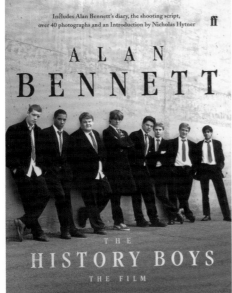

Includes Alan Bennett's diary, the shooting script,
over 40 photographs and an Introduction by Nicholas Hytner

ff

ALAN
BENNETT

THE
HISTORY BOYS
THE FILM

©History Boys Ltd – photo: Alex Bailey
Reproduced by kind permission of Faber and Faber

However, I suggest it would also result
in a tedious collection of still photography.
A good stills photographer does spend
a lot of time photographing around the
movie camera, replicating similar shots
to the actual film, but this is only the
foundation on which to build on, it is
the stills photographer's expert eye,
and ability, that will expand this into an
exciting and impressive collection of
stills from a movie.

The romantic photograph is always required for a film with a love interest.

Ewan McGregor and
Renée Zellweger
in Miss Potter

©Miss Potter Inc. - photo: Alex Bailey

DIGITAL RAW FILE 320ISO 85MM 1/100 F3.5 3200K

KODAK PORTRA 1000ISO 135MM 1/125 F5

**Keira Knightley and
Matthew Macfadyen
in Pride and Prejudice**

©2005 Focus Features - photo: Alex Bailey
Courtesy of Universal Studios Licensing LLLP

**Cate Blanchett
and Joseph Fiennes
in Elizabeth**

©1998 Universal City Studios, Inc.
Photo: Alex Bailey
Courtesy of Universal Studios Licensing LLLP

KODAK EPL 105MM **1/500** F5

Before a film starts shooting the stills photographer generally gets a few preparation (prep) days. This is a good chance to touch base with anyone interested in what the stills photographer will be producing. More often than not this is the film's distributors or rather their marketing and publicity departments. Key images, identified from the script, can be agreed upon, as can other photographic expectations, in other words a visual brief is outlined. Looking at a film's storyboard, if one is available, can be visually very helpful at this time, or any other visual references used for creative inspiration by the film-makers.

Prep days are also a good opportunity to look around a few of a film's numerous departments to generate some ideas. The art department is often visually informative in the lead up to a film shooting. Art departments often have excellent scale models, texture references and drawings of sets in various stages of construction. The costume department is also worth a visit, as is the hair and make-up department. Visiting other departments is also a good opportunity to break the ice with co-workers before arriving on set for the first take.

On larger productions, photographs of 'hero' costumes and props are particularly requested as they may be needed for model making and packaging if there is to be related merchandising for a film.

Sometimes photographs that will be used as props or set dressing in the film are required, the stills photographer may well be asked to shoot these photos.

Images of sets in various stages of construction, their related drawn plans and scale models are necessary for a film that is likely to publish a making of book. These images can also service articles in magazines that take the behind the scenes angle.

Stills photographers do not provide photos for continuity purposes. All the departments needing continuity photos cater for their own needs, save only on a rare occasion when an exacting

DIGITAL RAW FILE 200ISO 145MM 1/250 F6.3 5300K

Brenda Blethyn and Keira Knightley
in Pride and Prejudice

KODAK PORTA 640ISO 105MM 1/125 F5

Profile two shots with the subjects facing the same way convey a close, but not necessarily intimate relationship between characters.

Natalie Portman and Scarlett Johansson in The Other Boleyn Girl

DIGITAL RAW FILE 640ISO 35MM
1/160 F5 5300K

DIGITAL RAW FILE 320ISO 85MM 1/100 F3.5 3200K

**Ewan McGregor
and Renée Zellweger
in Miss Potter**

Descriptive stills are very desirable;
this uncomplicated image describes
the story of Miss Potter and Mr Warne,
her publisher, very well.

©Miss Potter Inc. - photo: Alex Bailey

degree of very close-up detail is needed
that would benefit from a very high
resolution image, this happens maybe
once or twice on your average film.

All the photography from a film is
individually numbered and contact
sheeted. Typically the publicity office

has a set of contact sheets and there
will be the need for at least another one
or two sets for actors stills approval,
the director and producer may require
a set, and then, if the distributors are
already actively involved they will
probably want a couple of sets too,
for their marketing department.

Angelina Jolie in Lara Croft Tomb Raider:
The Cradle of Life
on set Specials

The scene that resulted in me getting this image was for
a commercial for the film, not a common element to
shoot during the filming but equally not totally unusual;
the call sheet described it as: Iconic footage of Lara Croft
in silver wet suit. I took my medium format Pentax shot
1 roll of film and it made the poster.

Lara Croft Tomb Raider: The Cradle of Life
©Courtesy of Paramount Pictures
Photo: Alex Bailey

A real task in itself, producing all that material, not something the stills photographer has time for, and results in the need for a reliable specialist lab such as www.loftyslab.co.uk.

At the end of a stills assignment, all the original photography is handed over to the film-makers who retain copyright.

It is common practice that the stills photographer is allowed to keep approved stills for their portfolio, and own promotional use. Although, I would not recommend posting any of these images to a web site prior to a film's release, in danger of leaving yourself vulnerable to pre-empting a distributor's planned marketing campaign, should an image be lifted from your web site and published elsewhere.

Not strictly speaking part of the stills photographer's brief, but nonetheless expected, are the happy snaps. Photographs of the various visitors that pop in on a film set, (from royalty and celebrities to the crew members family) is generally the responsibility of the stills photographer, the only person allowed to take pictures on the set, mainly for reasons of copyright and security.

So expect to be summoned for the happy snaps!

**Gerard Butler
in The Phantom of the Opera**

©Really Useful Films and Scion Films
Phantom Productions Partnership, 2004
Photo: Alex Bailey

KODAK FRI 320T 640ISO 85MM 1/100 F4.5

KODAK EPP RATED @ 50ISO **X PROCESSED** 17MM **1/125** F5

Michael Stevenson
2nd assistant director, 2nd unit
Atonement

Apart from the fact the film-makers wanted to
shoot this scene with the benefit of the afternoon
light, it took all day to organise and position
the several thousand extras.

Setting the Scene

In much the same way as an understanding of the mechanics of film production is important, even more so is an in-depth knowledge of the workings of a film set and the relationships that the stills photographer will need to develop.

The stills photographer must have an appreciation of their fellow crew members' jobs, and the way they operate, as well as an excellent working relationship with them.

There is a certain mystique that surrounds a film set. I tend to think that this is mainly due to the lack of straightforward first-hand information available, coupled with the general public's desire to elevate most media related industries into the realms of something extraordinary.

Defined by an infatuation with anything celebrity related. In fact, from my experience in working in the film industry, it is similar to most regular places of employment. A film production is structured in very much the same way to most businesses. I liken it to a pyramid with the overall bosses, the producers, directors and the actors at the top, followed by the heads of departments with each of their related family trees and staff of varying status and experience mushrooming below them.

Everyone involved with the making of a film, across the whole board, from actors to the crew, are all very hard working determined individuals, who, have only got (and stayed) where they are by working at it for many years. The only grey area is on the issue of talent, a very difficult attribute to quantify. The word talent, or talented, is often bestowed on a cross section of individuals in the film business from actors and directors to costume designers and cameramen plus everyone in-between and either side.

DIGITAL RAW FILE 500ISO **135MM** 1/100 **F5** 3200K

Sebastian Barraclough B camera clapper
loader - Miss Potter

In this picture Sebastian is standing on the actor's mark
with the board and torch so the focus puller can check
the sharps, this helps me to compose my shot and
check focus as well. Plus Seb's Mum gets a nice
photo for the mantle piece.

©Miss Potter Inc. - photo: Alex Bailey

DIGITAL RAW FILE 200ISO 50MM 1/320 F5 5900K

David Smith Gaffer
Miss Potter

David is using a panaglass to check the sun
and cloud position, so as to identify a long
enough window of consistent light for a take.

©Miss Potter Inc. - photo: Alex Bailey

It is safe to say that talent alone does not make a career in the movies. Anyone who has got anywhere in the film biz has done it by sheer determination, hard work, and talent. All the people at the so-called 'sharp end' i.e. around the movie camera, director, continuity, boom op, make-up, costume, hair, stills photographer and many more conduct themselves very professionally and are respectful of each other, allowing each and all to perform their task un-hindered, if a little hassled sometimes!

The financial remuneration between members of the same crew can, and usually is, quite contrasting, but again that is the same as most other industries where people of varying experience and expertise work in close proximity to one another.

I have always been politely and very tolerably accepted on film sets, only occasionally encountering a lack of understanding of the importance of what I do. I think that this is partly due to the fact that most of the crew are only concerned with the business of making the film. Unlike the stills photographer whose work is an investment for the future, mainly to be used after the film is completed.

DIGITAL RAW FILE 125ISO 17MM 1/320 F5.6 5300K

Crew Atonement

Camera track on a rostrum with the dolly and
camera. The track must be very level with no bumps;
there is a real skill in laying track, which is done by
the grip and standbys.

A film is a 'product', which will require marketing and the quality of that campaign
is likely to have a direct effect on its commercial success.

Individual crew members do not directly benefit financially from the revenue
generated from a film, rather their desirability increasing due to their association
with successful projects, possibly enabling them to charge higher fees for their
services in the future.

DIGITAL RAW FILE 250ISO 26MM 1/80 F4 5300K

Peter Robertson
camera/Steadicam operator
Atonement

Always a new idea – they nicknamed this, sparkplug
cam – essentially a hand-held movie camera effect.

©2007 Focus Features - photo: Alex Bailey
Courtesy of Universal Studios Licensing LLLP

DIGITAL RAW FILE 320ISO **17MM** 1/160 **F5.6** 5500K

Crew Atonement

Here the Steadicam operator is filming off the back of a low-loader imitating the artist's point of view from a bus as it pulls away.

©2007 Focus Features - photo: Alex Bailey
Courtesy of Universal Studios Licensing LLLP

On the basis that a stills photographer is providing one of the key marketing ingredients, it is essential they have the best un-hindered access to the set as possible, enabling them to get the quality and quantity of shots needed.

Generally, the stills photographer experiences a great deal of co-operation on set to the point whereby a complete scene can be performed for the benefit of the stills person (go-again for stills please!). In this instance, the movie camera is withdrawn so the stills photographer has clear access to the set and actors, enabling them to shoot the scene at will. Often the director helps by motivating and asking the actors to repeat part of a scene that lends itself to definitive stills. Whilst the 1st assistant director keeps a close eye on the time, always conscious to be 'moving on' in order to complete the day's work.

When arriving on set for the first time, it is a good idea to re-introduce yourself to the director. It may have been weeks since you last met. He or she has probably met tens, if not hundreds, of crew, cast and supporting artists since then. It is polite and prudent to remind them who you are and what you do if it is not obvious by the camera, or two, slung round your neck.

At the same time single out the 1st AD. You probably recognize them by their voice first, as they are the person who runs the set and therefore spends the majority of their time speaking into a walkie-talkie and whose orders and enquiries you have heard reverberating around the production offices (via the walkie-talkie) and set from the minute you arrived. The 1st AD's job is to run the 'floor' from a technical aspect, lights, camera, action etc. The creative side is the director's responsibility. The 1st AD has a vested interest in who is on set at any one time (crew included); anything or anyone that prevents the smooth running of the shooting day, potentially jeopardizing the films tight schedule, is a concern to them.

The 1st AD is a person you really want on your side, or at least not against you.

They are constantly concerned about the organization of the set and getting the actors in front of the camera promptly, when required.

Peter Robertson camera/Steadicam operator Gary Hutchings grip & crew Atonement

They call this a rickshaw cam, yet another way of making the movie camera mobile.

DIGITAL RAW FILE 400ISO **17MM** 1/125 **F5.6** 5500K

To do this they will rely heavily on the 2nd AD, communicating regularly, with each other, via their walkie-talkies. The 2nd AD is based close to the artists' dressing rooms breathing politely down the necks of the actors and the various departments required in dressing and making-up the artist to get them to the set ready to shoot the moment they are needed. The 2nd AD can be very helpful to a stills photographer, particularly if and when additional photography is required. They are the person that can often find windows of opportunity, with the 1st AD's blessing, during the filming day, when an actor is made-up and in costume but not needed on set, probably because they are 'turning around' on set or the actor has completed their scene, therefore being available for a few stills off set somewhere.

After touching base again with the director, and breaking the ice with the 1st and 2nd AD, it is sensible to introduce oneself to other key players around the movie camera: 3rd ADs, floor runners, DOP, cameraman, focus puller, clapper loader, grip, best boy, continuity, sound recordist and boom op.

Josh Robertson 1st AD
Keira Knightley & Saoirse Ronan
Atonement

Josh shielding the actors from the sun, on the hottest day of the year, for real. Ironic if you know the story

DIGITAL RAW FILE 200ISO **80MM** 1/320 **F8** 5300K

DIGITAL RAW FILE HI-2ISO **17MM** 1/80 **F3.2** 3300K

Keira Knightley and James McAvoy in Atonement

A good working relationship with cast and crew alike is very important especially with so much equipment in so many small spaces. Mind that eyeline!

These are the colleagues whose cooperation will make the difference between an easy and a hard life for the stills photographer when going about the daily business of shooting stills. An excellent working relationship and understanding of your co-workers responsibilities, coupled with a sympathetic attitude to the mechanics of a working film set, is half the story. The other half is the relationship between the stills photographer and the actors.

Fact: You have to get the shots and there is only one way, by pointing the camera at the artists and pressing the button, like any subject! This a stills photographer will be doing for several months and there is no way the right images will be achieved unless a good working relationship is developed, and maintained, between themselves and the artists.

The relationship between a photographer and those they photograph has been spoken and written about endlessly. I believe in the context of the film business, like so many aspects, it is best approached head on. My best advice is to clear the air regarding an actor's attitude to being photographed on and off the set, during rehearsals and at candid moments, prior to them arriving on set for the first time. Most actors are very approachable, either directly or via their assistant (if they have one), or ask one of the producers to make an introduction, something they are more than happy to do.

In my experience, there does not seem to be any hard and fast rules. Some actors prefer to be photographed during an actual take as they feel they are giving their best performance, with the reassurance the technicalities will be correct, namely lighting, hair, make-up and costume.

Keira Knightley in Atonement

All hands on deck or should I say neck, as the costume department fix Keira Knightely's necklace. Made a great magazine photo!

DIGITAL RAW FILE 250ISO 35MM 1/80 F4.5 5300K

DIGITAL RAW FILE 400ISO **17MM** 1/125 **F8** 5300K

Benedict Cumberbatch
in Atonement

Just keeping my eyes open and camera ready for
those moments that add the variety and extra interest
to the stills photography.

DIGITAL RAW FILE 320ISO 35MM 1/100 F5.6 6300K

On the other hand, some actors positively find a stills camera distracting and will only allow images to be taken during rehearsals. This requires the stills photographer to be more attentive regarding the details, hair, make-up and costume etc. and conscious that the performance is animated and conveys the emotion of the scene when it is filmed. In reality, one often finds a happy medium of photographing both rehearsals and takes. Deliberate shots during rehearsals or candid moments make excellent publicity photos ideal for magazines and web sites.

Although the bulk of the imagery required does need to be perfect photos of the actors performing in a scene.

A great deal of sensitivity is required at all times, even during candid moments. Constantly clicking and intrusive stills photographers have a habit of being asked to leave the set and come back later, as even if the actors are not fed up with the stills photographer's unsympathetic intrusion, then the director has got tired of the sound of the stills camera, endlessly clicking away in their headphones.

DIGITAL RAW FILE 640ISO **17MM** 1/125 **F9** 5900K

**Benedict Cumberbatch, Juno Temple,
Amanda Trewin & Suzanne Mills**
Atonement

There is always a photo on a film set; the contrast
of clothing in this shot adds to the intrigue.

This is not ideal, as in order to anticipate and record the best images, the stills photographer needs to be adjacent, pretty much most of the time, watching and weighing up all the potential photo opportunities.

Always behave professionally. Tread cautiously and address any issues that individual actors may have with being photographed, before they escalate, due to a lack of communication, into a problem.

If this does happen, or one experiences difficulties with an actor or indeed any crew member, the answer is to consult the producer who will invariably smooth things over.

I strongly recommend common sense at all times. If a scene is particularly emotional or challenging for example, then find an appropriate moment to ask an actor or the director about their opinion on images from the scene and how best to achieve them.

DIGITAL RAW FILE 500ISO 85MM 1/100 **F3.2** 5500K

A major concern to an actor is their eyeline.
The movie camera films as an invisible
observer therefore an actor avoids looking
directly into its lens, but, they are often
delivering their lines or directing their
performance very close to the lens axis,
any movement or direct eye contact in this
area is extremely distracting, annoying
and irritating to them.

A nuisance really, as this is where the
stills photographer spends a lot of
time photographing from! It is usual
practice to 'clear the eyelines',

a phrase often announced by the 1st
AD that should not be directed at the
stills photographer, as they should know
better than to be in it!

*The art of a good stills photographer is
being there but nobody knows you are.*

Overall it is worth remembering that
ultimately an actor wants to be visually
well represented on screen, and in stills.

Joe Wright Director **Atonement**

Joe Wright checking the frame in camera.

©2007 Focus Features - photo: Alex Bailey
Courtesy of Universal Studios Licensing LLLP

DIGITAL RAW FILE 250ISO **24MM** 1/125 **F3.2** 5500K

DIGITAL RAW FILE 500ISO 26MM 1/80 F5 5300K

Jennie Paddon, 2nd assistant camera

Atonement

Just shoot! The context, expression and lighting
says photograph me so I do.

Directors are very often sympathetic to the stills photographer, particularly when it comes to covering sensitive scenes for example the 'closed set' an expression used to restrict access to a scene that due to its content discretion is required (love scenes or nudity - definitely ask before entering!). The director's close relationship with the actors means that a stills photographer can ask them to assist in extracting key images from scenes that are awkward to cover.

Film sets are usually 'tight for space' with the shooting crew diplomatically vying for space. Occasionally the stills photographer finds the director wants to occupy the same prime position adjacent to the movie camera. However, the director spends the majority of their time in front of the playback monitors (video village), seeing the shot as it might appear on screen.

When the stills photographer, in their judgment, needs to have the scene photographed for stills it is the 1st AD that the stills photographer will turn to. They and they alone, control the set (diplomatically behind the director). At the end of a take the 1st AD will call a halt to proceeding, announcing: 'go again for stills', the whole scene will be played through for the benefit of the stills photographer to capture the key moments that they were unable to capture during the take.

DIGITAL RAW FILE 200ISO 200MM 1/250 F5 5300K

DIGITAL RAW FILE 500ISO 22MM 1/80 F4.5 5600K

This may have been for a number of reasons, perhaps because of the sensitivity of the scene, or maybe the set was very restrictive and the movie camera or sound boom intruded into the stills photographer's frame to the point where a well-composed poignant shot was not possible at the crucial moment.

To recap, the director, actors and the 1st and 2nd ADs are the most important people to start a good working relationship with, very closely followed by the members of the camera department.

The movie camera itself is a substantial piece of equipment, mounted on a tripod or dolly with a camera operator

and probably a grip operating the dolly, (tracking and jibbing) and the focus puller doing the sharps. These three or four people are working in close harmony, as most shots will require them to perform various functions in conjunction with each other, silently, as sound is being recorded.

In addition, amongst this close-knit huddle, weaving their way in and out is the stills photographer. Obscuring one of the team's sight of their reference marks or accidental jogging is totally unacceptable.

These lads and lasses are those whom the stills photographer will have the closest relationship with, as it is their feet the stills photographer will nearly be treading on whilst tiptoeing around the movie camera, getting the best shots and vantage points to shoot from. Their cooperation and sympathetic attitude to the stills photographer can mean the difference between getting a good clean shot of the action or no shot at all.

The person who makes the biggest difference to the stills photographer is the focus puller. They are required to focus the movie camera while it is filming. This is done without being able to look down the lens, as the camera operator is looking through the viewfinder following the action by panning and tilting the camera head. No mean feat, for the focus puller, achieved by accurate measurements in rehearsals, helped by focus marks (chalk, tape or 'sausages') put down on the floor as a reference in the takes.

It is amazing that any form of autofocus has not yet been perfected for movie cameras. This is partly due to the creative benefit of being able to shift the plane of focus during a shot; typically, in a dialogue scene for example where the focus can be shifted between two people talking in profile as each one speaks.

DIGITAL RAW FILE 200ISO **50MM** 1/320 **F5** 5900K

Mark Milsome A camera focus puller
Miss Potter

Checking the gate – Mark is holding up the camera's
film gate and checking for obstructions that would
register on the exposed negative. If he finds
anything he will announce 'hair in the gate' and they
will 'go again'.

DIGITAL RAW FILE 500ISO **50MM** 1/80 **F4** 5600K

Chris Atkinson 2nd boom operator
Atonement

Advice: never arm wrestle with a boom operator,
at least not for money.

On the basis that the action, and consequently the lighting and the physical set itself, are for the movie camera to film, the best place for the stills photographer to be during a take is very close to the movie camera. Enjoying the same point of view, this results in the stills photographer being shoulder to shoulder with the focus puller and camera operator.

The boom op, who wields a long pole, with a microphone at the end and trails a cable attached to the sound mixing desk, is another crew member whose mutual co-operation the stills photographer will benefit from. Often their physicality can act as a shield to the stills photographer's presence and in the same way the stills photographer finds themselves in very close proximity to the camera crew the same can be said of the boom op.

There are others that the stills photographer should be aware may also require a clean sight of the action, so their view should not be obstructed. The continuity person checking the smallest details as a scene is performed repeatedly, various lighting personnel who may be timing lighting queues on the arrival of actors at particular marks or on occasions, a special effects operator who again may be timing effects at certain crucial moments during a take.

DIGITAL RAW FILE 200ISO **100MM** 1/320 **F5** 5500K

The usual pattern to a filming day is for the director to have a short private rehearsal with the actors before each scene - blocking through. Then the crew is invited in for a viewing rehearsal, this is when the director, director of photography and camera operator will then decide how many 'set-ups' the scene will be broken down into. They will agree on lens size and camera moves, such as tracking or cranes, whether to shoot off the dolly, on sticks, baby legs, hand-held or with a Steadicam. A storyboard, if there is one, may be referred to at this point for guidance. Once the coverage has been decided, then the lighting, the most time consuming aspect of filming, will be completed. Most sets are pre-lit to save time, but there is a limit to how much pre-lighting can be done as until the scene is witnessed on the day, by the creative team, final decisions cannot be made as to the finer details. This is the time for other technicalities to be dealt with such as: radio microphoning the actors, setting-up video village, final touches to the set and rigging any special effects. All closely watched over by an anxious 1st AD as the time evaporates!

Miss Potter

A Panavision Supertechno crane that can extend 30 plus feet. It comes with at least 2/3 specialist operators. Often used for those close-up shots that then fly up in the air and zoom out to reveal, as in this case, a far-reaching view or landscape.

©Miss Potter Inc. - photo: Alex Bailey

KODAK PORTRA 320ISO 50MM 1/125 F5.6

*It is not the takes that take the time;
it is the time between the takes that
take the time...*

Each scene being broken down into
several set-ups, is in turn shot several
times (take 1, take 2, take 3), mainly for
the benefit of the actors performance,
with the director giving notes to the
artists after each take. Technical quality
is also a consideration, as most shots
require several camera movements,
perfection in the form of smoothness
and fluidity of the camera may take a
few attempts.

The director will probably ask to 'swing
a lens' at least once on each set-up and
'go again' several times. This gives the

stills photographer several bites at
the pie to get the required images by
shooting different sizes and angles
therefore extracting different elements
from a set-up. It is not at all unusual
to have a second or even a third movie
camera running at the same time,
referred to as the 'B' and 'C' camera,
picking out elements of the set-up
(cutaways) or shooting different lens
sizes to give extra footage to cut from
when editing. Each has their own
operator, focus puller and grip, add to
this the hair, make-up, costume,
lighting, art department and effects
personnel and it does not take long
for the set to get pretty crowded.

DIGITAL RAW FILE 320ISO **35MM** 1/125 **F5** 5500K

Joe Wright Director
Atonement

Joe Wright framing up another brilliantly
choreographed shot.

Miss Potter

DIGITAL RAW FILE 500ISO 80MM 1/320 F8 5300K

You know you've made it in the film biz when
you get a chair with your name on it.

I'm still waiting for mine!

A film set definitely does rely on the polite professional conduct of all involved and an understanding of what each individual's function and reason for being there is.

A few other tips and notes worth mentioning. It seems obvious to say but standing in front of lights, therefore shielding or casting shadows on the set, or the actors, is a no no. Bare in mind that with so much equipment on a set there is a lot of cabling, some of which is trailed along during a take, in particular the boom operator's sound cable, so avoid treading on and tripping over cables in general. Large camera bags are best kept well to the side of the set. Stills cameras left lying around on set are vulnerable to damage and embarrassing if they end up in the shot. And as the props man will be happy to tell you the actors chairs are for them to sit in so bring your own if you want to take the weight of your feet!

KODAK EPP 120 MAMIYA RZ 50MM 1/500 **F16** STROBE

Doing it

How a photographer approaches any assignment is a personal issue. We are all individuals and that is reflected in our own style of photography.

This book is based on my own experiences of working in the film and TV business, for more than sixteen years, and a photographic career than now spans twenty five plus years.

No doubt, many similarities exist between my approach and experiences to others working in the same genre. However, this chapter very much reflects my individual approach to photography, and in particular film assignments.

Noah Taylor in Lara Croft:Tomb Raider
Specials Shoot

Lara Croft: Tomb Raider
©Courtesy of Paramount Pictures
Photo: Alex Bailey

The starting point is having a comprehensive in-depth technical knowledge of my equipment, to the point whereby operating it has become completely second nature.

The camera is an extension of the body; I expect it to behave in the same way as my hand does for example, instinctively.

In my mind's eye I can then pre-visualize the possibilities and restraints of a frame, allowing me to concentrate on capturing that key moment within, so that afterwards, when I study the image, it is precisely what was intended.

Easier said than done, and only becomes reliably achievable after years of taking photographs, the definition of a truly professional and competent photographer.

How one deals daily with the issues of going about the task of being a photographer on a film set is very individual. There are certainly advantages and disadvantages to being predominately a department of one. Not least, that no one knows quite where you stand in the film's hierarchy (an advantage) you are seen to have a relationship with the management but the mechanics of performing your job means you spend the majority of your time on the shop floor. A sometimes isolated existence being essentially a department of one (a disadvantage?): no particular conclusion: The stills photographer is unquantifiable and independent.

The stills photographer spends the majority of their time working on or close to the set: whilst filming is taking place, and different shots are being set up. What it comes down to is finding a balance between not missing any key moments with not being overly intrusive or obvious on the set . How I achieve this is by waiting in the wings, remaining on the periphery of the set, keeping a watchful eye for potential photo opportunities. Waiting whilst the crew set up, ready to capture a few golden moments, whenever a chance arises, and judging when to stake my claim on the set, in the anticipation of the actors arriving and the proceedings getting under way for the main event: The scene itself.

'There is always a photo', a motto I remind myself of all the time, when working.

Film sets, by their very nature, are full of photo ops. Of course, you have actors

DIGITAL RAW FILE 320ISO 24MM 1/160 F4.5 5300K

Saoirse Ronan and James McAvoy
in Atonement

In order to get this shot in a tight doorway I had
to be in the exact same position as the movie
camera, a prime example of 'go again for stills'.

Cillian Murphy in Sunshine

Snatched during filming, the tight lens just
caught the suspense and horror in the eyes,
focused by the frame made by the hand
and window.

Shauna Macdonald
in The Descent

Abstract horror with real emotion, this became
a defining image for this movie.

Michelle Yeoh in Sunshine

Capturing shock moments can be hard, the framing in of the flames helped to describe the reason for the horror.

DIGITAL RAW FILE 400ISO 200MM 1/320 F5 4300K

KODAK PORTA 1600ISO 135MM 1/250 F2.8

in costume beautifully made-up and elaborate sets to photograph them in. One is often surrounded by stimulating locations, coupled with the juxtaposition of all the technical equipment, which is visually interesting in its own right. The challenge is to represent this three dimensional world in a two dimensional format that conveys an exciting and informative fact - not easy - experience certainly counts for a lot by developing ones visual literacy. In the first instance for me, this started with closely studying the work of other photographers and painters. This then graduated into

Saoirse Ronan in Atonement

The human window on the world. Eyes are fascinating and an obsession with a lot of film-makers and photographers, me included.

©2007 Focus Features - photo: Alex Bailey
Courtesy of Universal Studios Licensing LLLP

Jude Law in Enemy at the Gates

Still about the eyes but the picture needs the hint of fingers in the frame to fully explain the emotion: thoughtfulness. Try cropping out just the fingers with a piece of paper, the message is lost. Remember most stills are seen full frame, with so many images one could never organise or add cropping instructions, so these decisions to decide what to, and not to, include are made in the instance and stay with the film still forever.

©MM by MP Film Management DOS Productions GmbH & Co. KG. All Rights Reserved.
Photo: Alex Bailey

benefiting from just getting out there and taking a lot of photographs, printing them myself, analyzing and being self-critical by comparison, and then considering how best I could improve what I was shooting.

A very good exercise for improving composition is working off a tripod from a fixed point of view, for example by photographing a still life. Being able to move and consider the position of component parts of a composition, will help later when framing, in or out, elements surrounding an actor on set to improve the overall balance of a shot.

I always keep a number of key compositional guidelines in mind such as the three part rule, which works on

KODAK PORTRA 800ISO 35MM 1/125 F4

the principle of dividing your frame into three component parts, typically foreground, middle ground, and distant and balancing them in the frame.

Using parts of a set, or positioning myself where objects or component parts of an image lead you in and out of a picture, is a tried and tested technique; in much, the same way a landscape painter might use a road or hedge to guide you through a painting.

Frames within frames, a basic compositional technique that can be used to great effect.

Diagonals in an image give the feeling of movement, a well-known fact.

The use of pattern in an image, or framing areas to extract a pattern from a scene is visually arresting.

Technical control is important, particularly applied when using depth of field to emphasize part of an image like separating an actor's face from the surrounding distractions by using a shallow depth of field and a long lens.

The deliberate use of movement in an image adds intrigue and urgency.

KODAK PORTRA 800ISO 85MM 1/125 F4

Andrew Knott in The History Boys
Set up stills

©History Boys Ltd – photo: Alex Bailey
By kind permission of Nicholas Hytner,
Damian Jones and Kevin Loader

An appreciation of light, both artificial and natural, is vital of course. Being able to exploit the lighting available can change a dull image into a stunner by changing ones angle to the light source, deliberate flare, backlighting and silhouetting are prime examples.

Point of view and the lens used, again, can radically alter the dynamics of a shot; low angles and wide lenses used close in are very effective, particularly good for drawing a viewer into a shot and making them feel engaged and involved with an image.

I even consider post-production when looking for shots, especially now with the advent of easy image manipulation via digital, looking for component parts probably from blue/green screen computer generated image sequences that could be put together later in the computer to form a completed image. A particular requirement for special effects movies where computer generated characters are involved.

When using film consider processing for creative effect, namely cross processing.

All these points have become second nature to me and are constantly rolling around in my head, conjuring up the best possibilities from any one given scene or situation.

Therefore when the long awaited moment eventually arrives and the actors are gathered to the set to rehearse, one final time, allowing the various technical departments to perfect their performance as well, the ante is raised.

KODAK EPL 35MM **1/60** F5

Daniel Craig in Some Voices

An arresting image that the producer told me
(several years later on another project) had
positively helped to get the film noticed, due to
its repeated publication.

©Dragon Pictures - photo: Alex Bailey

KODAK PORTRA 800ISO **180MM** 1/250 **F4**

**Cambodia during filming of
Lara Croft: Tomb Raider**

Depth of field, depth of dedication.

Lara Croft: Tomb Raider
©Courtesy of Paramount Pictures
Photo: Alex Bailey

Angelina Jolie in Lara Croft Tomb Raider: The Cradle of Life

A CGI sequence filmed against a green screen where the content carries enough interest that fancy composition is not required, helped though by the three-part rule, camera, Angelina Jolie and flag.

Lara Croft Tomb Raider: The Cradle of Life
©Courtesy of Paramount Pictures
Photo: Alex Bailey

As the stills photographer I have pre-conceived a number of potential images I wish to achieve from the scene. Now is the time for me to ensure I am ideally positioned to take advantage of the best angle to get the key shots. Most scenes lend themselves to at least one particular perfect moment, for which one must be totally prepared. With the benefit of maybe a couple of takes, and now with the security of instant viewing on a digital camera, alternative angles and shots can be weaned from a scene to the point that after several takes I am absolutely assured that all the possibilities have been extracted.

For myself, digital has been a revolution. No more worrying about processing problems or issues with exposure. I can also shoot the equivalent of five or six rolls of film without reloading during a long scene. This eliminates the concern associated

KODAK PORTRA 250ISO 85MM 1/125 F8

Atonement

A really strong diagonal adds the energy to this special effects shot on Atonement.

©2007 Focus Features - photo: Alex Bailey

Courtesy of Universal Studios Licensing LLLP

DIGITAL RAW FILE 800ISO **17MM** 1/125 **F3.5** 4200K

KODAK EPJ 320T **RATED @ 500ISO** 105MM **1/160** F4

Angelina Jolie in Lara Croft: Tomb Raider

A diagonal brings the feeling of movement

Lara Croft: Tomb Raider

©Courtesy of Paramount Pictures

Photo: Alex Bailey

with when the best time might be to use each one of my precious **thirty six** frames on a roll of film. Well done to whoever perfected digital cameras.

I have always felt a huge responsibility for producing the range of images relied upon so heavily by the publicity and marketing machine, which ultimately will be responsible for establishing a movie in a very competitive market place. This in turn has helped me to remain motivated and determined, on a day-to-day basis, in order to achieve the best possible results from any situation that I find myself in. This also leads me to constantly consider what more I can do to add to the photography that I will deliver at the end of an assignment.

Regularly producing the somewhat formulaic images, that are the bread and butter of any stills assignment, is the foundation to build on.

Essentially if a stills photographer positions themselves adjacent to the movie camera and shoots broadly what

KODAK TRI-X 320ISO 85MM 1/30 F8 DAYLIGHT + FLASH ON REAR CURTAIN SYNC AT F2.8

Jude Law in Enemy at the Gates

It took me weeks of trying to perfect this technique and make it reliable enough to risk trying it on the principal actors. Pin sharp in the face, the rest blurred by degrees and caught ideally with the background framing.

Atonement

Although there can be a lot going on in a scene from a film the movie camera has the advantage over stills of being continuous. Finding single shots that define a scene is hard, using a long lens here helped to compress a number of elements resulting in an image containing lots of information.

DIGITAL RAW FILE 320ISO **80MM** 1/320 **F6.3** 5600K

they shoot, they will achieve this basic collection of images required. However, what makes the difference between a reliable and a brilliant stills photographer is one key factor for me - 'the decisive moment' (this being the defining moment to take a photograph), a phrase synonymous with the photographer's photographer, Henri Cartier-Bresson. He is, in my opinion (and many others), the king of the decisive moment (his phrase anyway, I believe). It is he, who has been the greatest single influence on me as a photographer. Considering that, a still is art imitating life, when one looks at so many of his images it is as if they were shot the other way round, life imitating art. Like stills from a film, not taken from real life situations. Take time in studying the work of Henri Cartier-Bresson, a real artist.

DIGITAL RAW FILE 200ISO **35MM** 1/160 **F3.2** 4200K

Eddie Redmayne
in The Other Boleyn Girl

Always looking for those intriguing publishable shots.

I do believe that with practice, and careful analysis of the results, ones ability to anticipate the decisive moments definitely improves.

The very best stills photographers are those whose pictures show an actor animated and performing in the context of the film - decisive moments! This is ultimately qualified when one of these images becomes the key artwork or poster for a film.

A good way to educate your mind's eye to recognize decisive moments in films is to watch movies looking for them, when you think you see one freeze-frame and perhaps play the few frames either side. It soon becomes apparent how fleeting those tiny moments are. Although, as outlined in the previous chapter, the stills photographer is likely to have had several chances when the scene was being shot to capture these moments, providing they recognized the potential in the first place.

A quick tip here - I often find looking at the playback monitors, during a rehearsal, helps to pick out the key moments that will best describe a scene with a still image before the actual take.

I also adhere to the golden rule of press photography, which states that:

'if your pictures are not strong enough, then you are not close enough!'

A photographer must not be afraid to get involved, to get amongst the action.

With stills photography there is always a need for the establishing shot, the wide-angle view, but it is the close, tight intimate and animated shots that really make the grade.

All things considered, it is the animated and decisive images, with a good splattering of the more avant-garde and unusual shots that I yearn for on a film set, culminating in a collection of images that really define a movie in one shot, the quintessential still, the difference between a good and a great stills photographer.

Saoirse Ronan in Atonement

This image was shot through non-reflective glass, quite a complicated set-up for the movie camera and specific only to its lens, therefore no good for me during the take. Joe Wright, the director, was keen that I got a similar shot so after they had finished shooting on the movie camera the same set-up was replicated for me. He was right; this shot has been extensively used for the publicity.

DIGITAL RAW FILE 160ISO 85MM
1/320 **F5.6** 5900K

DIGITAL RAW FILE 500ISO **200MM** 1/250 **F4.5** 6300K

A Dior net (stocking!) for softening the image,
a polarizer to saturate it, a neutral density filter to keep
the stop wide and a Cyan filter for 'the look' or if it is
digital – do it in post – never – let's not lose the art!

Equipment

I tend to believe that there is a bit of an anorak in all us photographers and I am no exception.

I have always had an appetite for things technical, but I am firmly of the opinion that this is purely a means to an end. Ultimately the intuitive control of your equipment being that end.

Cameras and lenses are no more than tools of the trade. The latest state of the art camera does not make you a better photographer.

However, a lack of control and understanding, to the point where your equipment limits you, does make you a less able image-maker.

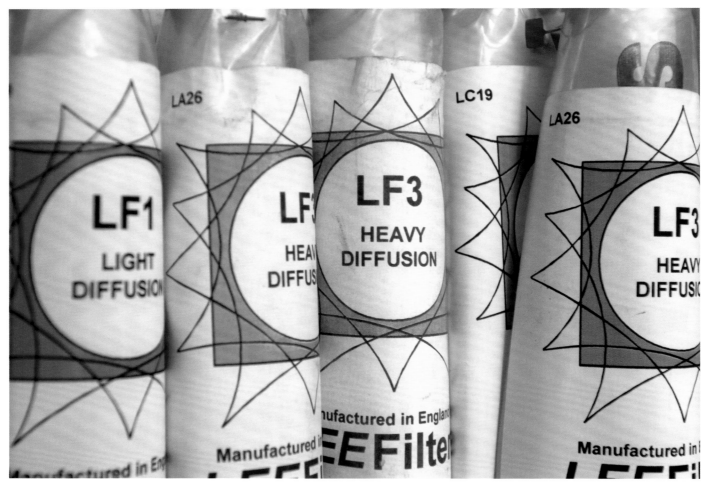

I was brought up on Nikon cameras, probably because of my press background where they were often the camera of choice, due, in part to their reputation for being virtually indestructible, especially the early models, coupled with the quality of their lenses.

I have remained faithful ever since, with absolutely no regret.

Never acquiring the latest model as soon as it is released, rather waiting until any initial problems are ironed out, if there are any.

On a film set, I work with two high-end digital SLR cameras, shooting in raw mode.

DIGITAL RAW FILE 800ISO **35MM** 1/125 **F5.6** 3200K

Diffusion.

DIGITAL RAW FILE 800ISO **26MM** 1/60 **F2.8** 3200K

So many cables on a film set where do they all lead?

It is worth mentioning here the use of a piece of equipment called a blimp. This is a sound proof box that a stills camera sits in allowing a photographer to shoot during takes silently (or nearly), without the noise of the camera being picked up by the sound recordist or heard by the actors, therefore lessening the possibility of any distraction during a take, a very useful and effective tool in the right hands.

One camera spends most of its time inside the blimp, which the design and mechanics of using is best accommodated by prime lenses. I use auto or manual focus lens mode as the situation dictates, manual focus mode giving me control over the exact plane of sharpness and where I place it, without compromising my composition.

On the blimped camera, I will invariably use a 35, 50, 85 and 105mm lens broadly following a similar pattern to the lens sizes the movie camera shoots with. The association with the movie camera lens, or frame size, is because the set, lighting and artists performance is structured to the movie camera's field of view, so it makes sense that I would look for images within the same parameters.

Beyond these boundaries, my frame would be 'off set'; I would be unlikely to capture the pivotal part of an artist's performance in a particular scene.

The second camera body I use in an opportunist way to capture additional moments, say during a rehearsal or at the end of a take, normally when I have identified a good shot that is not best

DIGITAL RAW FILE 640ISO **22MM** 1/100 **F4.5** 3200K

Lights

framed on the blimped camera. On the second camera body, I tend to use zoom lenses namely a 17-55mm f2.8 and an 80-200mm f2.8.

Ninety-nine per cent of the time, I use my cameras in manual mode, choosing to set the stop and shutter speed myself, utilizing the in-camera light meter.

Due to the relatively low levels of light used in filming interior scenes, my cameras' light sensitivity is generally set at between 400-1000 iso, which dictates working at apertures of between 2.8 and 5.6 with appropriate shutter speeds to the lens in use.

Exterior shooting gives me more flexibility and freedom with my iso, shutter speeds and apertures, the priority being a combination that gives me the highest resolution.

Nowadays, with such fantastically accurate in-camera light metering, backed up with histograms and the ability to view an image immediately, there is no great need for an independent hand-held light meter, although I do still keep two in the camera bag (a spot and an ambient meter) for the occasional reassurance that my camera metering is 100% accurate. I do also carry a colour temperature meter for awkward times, when the colour temperature is not obvious and confirmation is needed, allowing me to exactly match the colour temperature with the camera, as, most high-end digital cameras allow you to manually set colour temperature (have a look in the instructions!).

DIGITAL RAW FILE 250ISO **35MM** 1/80 **F6.3** 4300K

Lenses

©imagebarn – photo: Alex Bailey

DIGITAL RAW FILE 200ISO **50MM** 1/100 **F5** 5500K

Focus marks.

Working in prime, (particularly 35, 50, 85, 105mm) lenses is a good discipline and certainly helps in preconceiving the composition of a frame, although this has been rather scuppered with the advent of digital and the associated magnification issues inherent with digital cameras, with the exception of full frame digital cameras.

Interestingly when I look at meta data, on images taken using my zoom lenses, it surprises me how often the lens size used equates to the same or very close to my favoured prime lens size. Conclusion: That even without the restraints of a fixed lens, my eyes are trained to particular frame sizes, namely a 35, 50, 85 or 105mm lenses' field of view.

The digitization of images has been a revolution, not least for the advantages it has brought with the 'darkroom on a desk' phenomenon. The ability to easily adjust and manipulate an image combined with the quality of output printers, and the exciting range of surfaces available to print on, has positively enhanced photography.

However, for movie work I still occasionally use film cameras. This is due to two reasons, firstly the alternative formats available only in film cameras such as panoramic (a natural shape for film related work on the basis movies are shot in a cinematic format) and secondly the ethereal quality that shooting on film brings. From a creative point of view, I like the detached quality of film, it does feel magical, a separate world, unlike digital that both in the moving image and in stills, seems very in your face, true to life.

I suspect that photographers working in the film industry will always have the need to shoot some film, even if the majority of assignments are carried out digitally, for the same reasons the film-makers have their preference between the two, namely the desired creative appearance of a particular production.

There is often a need, for reasons of resolution, to use a larger format on set, particularly when shooting crowd scenes or substantial sets. My preference in these situations is a film camera, due to their reliability, simplicity and robust nature. Nothing is easier than a roll of film and a manual medium format camera.

In the same way, the death of black and white photography has been announced several times during my photographic career, but always enjoys a renaissance.

In my opinion, film based photography is destined for the same future; in fact, it will probably never entirely go away, please.

As far as other photographic gadgets and gismos are concerned, I do not really get involved, my overall approach to photography is quite purist.

My camera bags contain cameras, lenses, two light meters, a colour temperature meter, and a portable flash for the 'off set happy snap', the one per cent of time when I do not set the stop and shutter speed manually, preferring to use the camera in program mode. In addition, a couple of polarizing filters for daylight photography, when the benefits of a more saturated image and control of the highlights are desirable.

Oh yeah, and a cleaning kit and airbrush!

DIGITAL RAW FILE 125ISO **20MM** 1/800 **F5.6** 5500K

A Strada crane, comes with deckchair!

©imagebarn - photo: Alex Bailey

I tend to carry about 20 x 2 GB high write speed compact flash cards, which gives me at least 100 raw images on each card. Enough to cover a day, or two, on set shooting without connecting to the computer or other download device. Without also the risk of committing too many images to one card, safeguarding against image loss or damage. A reliable portable PC is a must these days with the associated card readers, hard drives, and a decent portable printer for chucking out a few proofs.

Generally, when shooting film stock, I use negative and transparency in equal amounts, influenced by the light and the preferred 'look' of the end result.

Track

DIGITAL RAW FILE 100ISO **100MM** 1/500 **F5.6** 5900K

KODAK PORTA 1000ISO 85MM 1/60 F4 3200K

Angelina Jolie in Lara Croft: Tomb Raider

Up-lighting adds intrigue.

Lara Croft: Tomb Raider

©Courtesy of Paramount Pictures

Photo: Alex Bailey

Lighting

The attributes of lighting could, and often does, demand the need for a whole book, which may only cover one aspect of lighting.

I have, in this publication, deliberately avoided delving too deeply into the technical aspects of photography, mainly because of the enormous quantity of books that already exist dealing with every conceivable technical issue and piece of equipment. However, do lookout, or pay particular attention to books covering the topics of: colour temperature, light meters and the inverse square law, all of which are intrinsic to understanding film lighting.

My primary concerns are with the practical application of light and how it effects, influences and enhances what I photograph.

DIGITAL RAW FILE 250ISO **135MM** 1/200 **F5.6** DAYLIGHT WHITE BALANCE 5500K

Cliff Curtis in Sunshine

Whilst the crew were setting up I shot this
through some gold strands that were being
used for lighting, to replicate the sun's rays.

The most dynamic light source of all, to me, is 'the sun'. After all, artificial lights are entirely controllable in their intensity, position and mould ability. The sun on the other hand is only adaptable by the use of reflectors and diffusible via silks and such like. Working with such a vibrant light source is by its very nature exciting.

Most of us photographers start by taking pictures in daylight, probably concentrating more on the subject than the illumination. Later we graduate into the studio where we begin to get to grips with controlling, and therefore understanding our light sources better. It is questionable how many actually return to study in more detail the fantastic qualities the sun can bring to images if controlled and manipulated in the right way, rather accepting the way it is, save only for a handful of photographers.

In order to appreciate fully my point I would suggest looking at (or rather I would hope re-looking at) two masters of natural light, Ansel Adams and Bill Brandt.

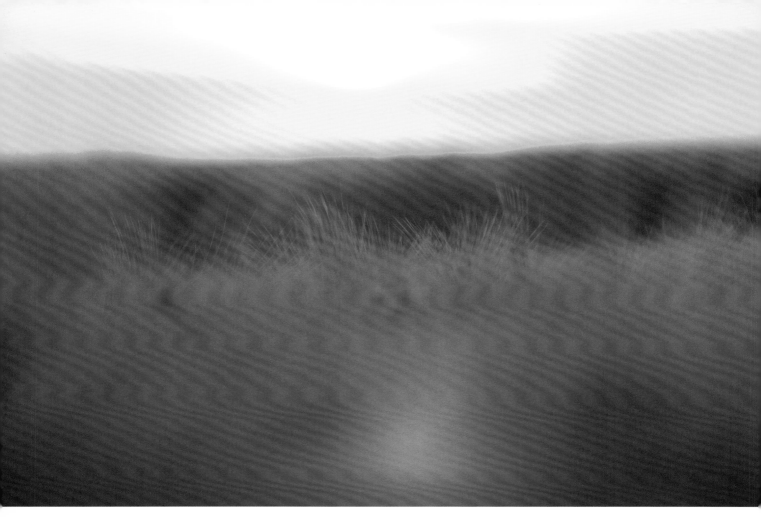

DIGITAL RAW FILE 800ISO **130MM** 1/250 **F5.6** 5500K

Summer sun over corn fields, the movement in tall corn made by the wind is beautiful; I did a whole series of images on this study.

©imagebarn - photo: Alex Bailey

It is the very nature of the sun, with its constantly changing relationship to our physical position, that brings the subtle, and not so subtle, visual changes that no other light source can. What other light source can give you such magical qualities first thing in the morning when it is turned on, through to such inspiring and evocative beauty as it fades in the evening? Certainly not your regular studio light.

The only way to really appreciate natural light is to study it, take time to look hard at how the sun's position radically alters a landscape and how the quality of the light changes during a day.

I recommend gaining knowledge in how best to control sunlight. Mainly achieved with the use of two pieces of equipment:

1. The reflector, in various degrees of intensity, ranging from the softer poly reflector to the direct mirror reflector with various stages in between, mainly for the benefit of 'fill in' lighting.

2. The diffuser, again in varying levels of diffusion accomplished by the use of varying light transmitting silks, tracing papers and gels, essentially to balance foreground and background illumination.

Whilst working in the Bahamas, on an American production I regularly witnessed the lighting of interior sets by means of reflected sunlight through windows and deliberate apertures cut in set walls and ceiling, a brilliant education for me! With a very reliable light source namely the sun, and a cloudless blue sky, very achievable.

When shooting artists with daylight I do not have any hard and fast rules.

I tend to prefer working with sunlight, when it is angled in the early morning or later on in the day. This is the same as most photographers, but only presents

Derelict tin mine near Zennor, Cornwall,
just playing with light, silhouette
and composition.

©imagebarn - photo: Alex Bailey

When out walking I have seen this image
through thickets several times, I like to
shoot things that just conjure an
emotion or illustrate an idea.

©imagebarn - photo: Alex Bailey

DIGITAL RAW FILE 125ISO **50MM** 1/250 **F16** 5500K

a small window of opportunity, probably a few minutes, maybe an hour at most, either end of the day.

Depending on the time of day, extent of cloud cover and where you are in the world, the qualities of a day's light is extremely variable. Generally during the middle part of a sunny day the light is at its brightest and most contrasting, but less easy to manipulate, fine for extracting details when contrast will enhance an image or add depth.

On an overcast day the general attributes of the light are described as flat. A soft overall illumination like this can be very workable and ideal for general photography when the concentration of the subject is of primary importance. When working with daylight I use a range of reflectors and flags, with knowledgeable hands to control them, all the time keeping a close eye on the light meter's reading.

As photographers we mainly opt to shoot either inside or out. In the context of working on film sets there is a halfway house, when typically, a set is lit on the inside to balance with daylight on the outside. A good example of this is when a scene requires an actor to be filmed looking out of a window across a live view. In this scenario the interior

daylight balanced (colour temperature 5500k) illumination needs to match the exterior's intensity. This is achieved by increasing the strength of the interior lighting and/or with the use of neutral density gels on the outside of the windows in varying thicknesses.

DIGITAL RAW FILE 250ISO **17MM** 1/400 **F6.3** 5500K

Looking for the silhouette here made
a picture from nothing.

©imagebarn - photo: Alex Bailey

The opposite of this is when we see an actor outside with buildings and their interiors, if relevant, in the background. Say an actor walking along a street at night, in this situation the artist in foreground will be lit by a tungsten light (3200k colour temperature) matching in intensity (by means of a fader) with the shop's interior tungsten lights (colour balance matched). The last couple of examples are a testimony to the multitude of lighting scenarios encountered when working in the film business, which are seemingly endless.

I cannot deny that by working with some excellent DOPs, in a vast range of lighting situations, my knowledge of using and controlling both natural and artificial light has been greatly enhanced by watching and learning from their techniques.

The first thing that really struck me lighting wise, when I first worked on interior film sets, was the enormous range of lighting equipment and paraphernalia used to mould the lighting. In addition to all the different shapes, sizes and combinations of lights used was the ancillary but very necessary component parts that either clip, hang or are inserted into or onto the lights.

With an equal amount of items that are positioned in front, held by frames or stands that help to adapt or balance the illumination and remarkably how

I can never resist shots like this when I see them; it is all about the light.

©imagebarn - photo: Alex Bailey

differently this equipment is utilized by individual DOPs. My advice is watch and learn from a film's DOP and the very knowledgeable people that support him, who should be looked on as allies, especially when it comes to borrowing equipment for extra stills shoots or leaving lights on to photograph a set over lunch or at the end of a filming day.

Consider transferring many of the lighting techniques you witness on a film set to the photo studio; this will vastly alter your perception of what can be achieved.

It does not take long to pick up the rudiments of using continuous lighting, opposed to what most photographers are used to working with, namely strobe or flash lighting. Especially if one makes use of the abundant amount of lighting equipment available on a film

DIGITAL RAW FILE 250ISO **16MM** 1/100 **F11** 5500K

Abstract shapes and light,

Roughtor on Bodmin Moor, Cornwall.

©imagebarn - photo: Alex Bailey

DIGITAL RAW FILE 640ISO **25MM** 1/250 **F8** 3200K

The vastness and range of lighting utilized in the film industry is mind blowing.

©imagebarn - photo: Alex Bailey

DIGITAL RAW FILE 250ISO **85MM** 1/800 **F6.3** 5900K

DIGITAL RAW FILE 800ISO **35MM** 1/125 **F14** 3200K

Photographs like this are symbolic of film-making.

They can get a light anywhere on a film set!

©imagebarn - photo: Alex Bailey

©imagebarn - photo: Alex Bailey

set, ultimately to the point where film lighting techniques can become part of ones repertoire of skills for the benefit of shooting stills.

In some ways it is strange that a photographer should operate in an environment where they have no control over the lighting or indeed for that matter any influence on the subject, save for

their own personal creative interpretation of what is presented to them.

That does not mean to say that any frustrations cannot be taken out by organizing and lighting your own shoots. Drawing on all those fabulous resources and talent available with, of course, the blessing of the production and generally the grateful thanks of the distributors'

marketing and publicity departments, who are always only too pleased to have additional material to compliment what is shot on set.

Where shooting with artificial light can sometimes become repetitive, I never tire of shooting using natural light probably because as no two days are the same, no two daylight shoots are the same.

DIGITAL RAW FILE 500ISO **85MM**1/250 **F8** 5500K

Rigging silk diffusers over a conservatory to make the daylight controllable.

©imagebarn - photo: Alex Bailey

Preparing lights for a night shoot, replicating moonlight from a high angle (80m+), hence the crane and blue gel over a tungsten light source.

©imagebarn - photo: Alex Bailey

DIGITAL RAW FILE 250ISO **80MM** 1/500 **F6.3** 6300K

DIGITAL RAW FILE 640ISO **26MM** 1/100 **F5** 3200K

Tungsten lights banks, that can pan, tilt, swing and be half or full power. Film lighting is so varied and versatile.

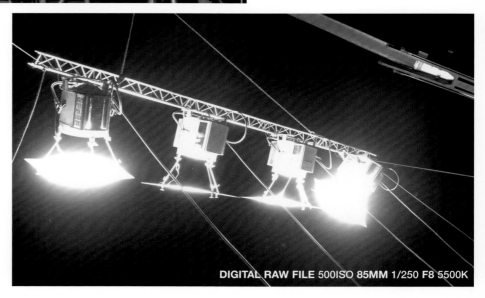

18kw lights on cable rig, night shoot London.

DIGITAL RAW FILE 500ISO **85MM** 1/250 **F8** 5500K

Crew photo from
Pride and Prejudice

On location, Stannage Edge,
Derbyshire Peak District.

©2005 Focus Features - photo: Alex Bailey
Courtesy of Universal Studios Licensing LLLP

KODAK PORTRA 160ISO 17MM 1/200 F11

On Location

At some point, most film productions go on location, mainly for the artistic visual benefits this will bring to a movie.

These locations may be at home or abroad or a combination of both.   Finding the right locations that are artistically, and physically, suitable can be challenging, this responsibility falls on the shoulders of the location manager and their staff under the guidance and input of the production designer, later rubber stamped by the director and the producers.

Organizing location shooting is a huge task, mainly coordinated by the production office with the help of the location department. It is likely that the production will hire local labour in each area they intend to shoot, who will support the film unit, both physically and in an advisory capacity.

DIGITAL RAW FILE 400ISO 35MM 1/125 F11 7700K

Renée Zellweger in Miss Potter

Pictures like this of the characters in context
with the relevant surroundings are a must.
The Lake District and Yorkshire dales were
very important to Beatrix Potter.

©Miss Potter Inc. - photo: Alex Bailey

Kate Hudson and Wes Bentley
in The Four Feathers

Photos with actors and iconic landmarks are
valuable publicity images. The Houses of
Parliament, London.

The production office organizes the travel
arrangements, flights, car hire, hotels
and catering etc for all the cast and
crew, on location. Carefully documented
equipment lists may be needed for
insurance, import/export declarations
and customs from the stills photographer,
something else the production office
can help with.

Reassurance that equipment will not be
damaged or lost in transit is achieved
by the use of good quality, well labelled
and robust flight cases, provided by
the photographer.

In order for the stills photographer
to operate efficiently when on location
they will have to be mobile and
independent. The best solution
is their own dedicated vehicle which
can act as a mobile office and
equipment store as well as transport
to and from the set.

Location shooting can be very tiring, not least because of the physical toll long distance travel takes, time differences and often the extreme conditions one is required to film in, deserts and up mountains for example.

Long filming days and six day working weeks are common practice.

Transportation, accommodation, catering and the general infrastructure needed for a film crew on location, is very expensive.

It is often the locations that make a film for the stills photographer. The opportunity to work outside, utilizing daylight and therefore not restricted by the slow pace that films often have in the studio, is a real relief. The location shooting of a film is normally the grander elements, the big scenes with lots of supporting artists, the action sequences, the beauty shots and so on. So much so that location filming often dictates the need for a stills assistant or additional photographer.

I love location shooting on movies; there is always so much visually to get your teeth into. Even the filming equipment goes up a gear with the use of large cranes, wind machines, cherry pickers etc. It is on location that big effects are often shot, explosions, car chases and battle sequences. At times in the studio, you might struggle on some scenes to find very much visually stimulating to photograph; on location, it is hard to stop shooting!

The day to day mechanics of performing the function of stills photographer will carry on in much the same way as in the studio, shooting alongside the movie camera when it is turning over, only the variation of images available increases dramatically both on and off the set.

Angkor Wat, Cambodia
during filming of Lara Croft:Tomb Raider

Location shots do not come much better than this, a fantastic set with a famous backdrop with the benefit of stunning light. Thanks Simon for running to get the Mamiya!

Lara Croft: Tomb Raider
©Courtesy of Paramount Pictures
Photo: Alex Bailey

KODAK PORTA 640ISO **200MM** 1/125 **F4**

On location in Kenya

A quintessential photo of Africa.

©Alex Bailey

If the physicality of a landscape or building is intrinsic to a film's story, ensure plenty of quality stills coverage, as it is surprising how often these images are incorporated into the key art (poster) for a movie.

Follow closely any instructions issued by the production office, usually attached to the call sheet; concerning your safety when on location, this may be for the reason of pyrotechnics, stunt routines or dangers relating to the location.

Stick to the path!

Alex Bailey on location in Cambodia

Do follow the instructions given on location, there were landmines to the side of this path, I know, I saw one. In town, I witnessed the dreadful consequences on young lives. Really scary! Support the ban landmines appeal. A hideous invention.

THE LIFE OF
BEATRIX POTTER IS
THE MOST ENCHANTING
TALE OF ALL.

RENÉE ZELLWEGER   EWAN McGREGOR

MISS POTTER

PG | TBC

PHOENIX PICTURES AND MOMENTUM PICTURES PRESENT IN ASSOCIATION WITH ISLE OF MAN FILM AND THE UK FILM COUNCIL A DAVID KIRSCHNER PRODUCTION IN ASSOCIATION WITH BBC FILMS
A CHRIS NOONAN FILM RENÉE ZELLWEGER EWAN McGREGOR "MISS POTTER" BILL PATERSON AND EMILY WATSON MUSIC BY NIGEL WESTLAKE ADDITIONAL MUSIC BY RACHEL PORTMAN EDITOR ROBIN SALES
COSTUME DESIGNER ANTHONY POWELL PRODUCTION DESIGNER MARTIN CHILDS DIRECTOR OF PHOTOGRAPHY ANDREW DUNN, BSC EXECUTIVE PRODUCERS RENÉE ZELLWEGER LOUIS PHILLIPS NIGEL WOOLL STEVE CHRISTIAN
PRODUCED BY MIKE MEDAVOY DAVID KIRSCHNER COREY SIENEGA ARNOLD W MESSER DAVID THWAITES WRITTEN BY RICHARD MALTBY, JR. DIRECTED BY CHRIS NOONAN

WWW.MISSPOTTERMOVIE.CO.UK

HASSELBLAD HD DIGITAL 100ISO **100MM** 1/500 **F22**

Specials

A specials photography shoot is commissioned, and paid for, separately from the film's stills budget, by the distributor's marketing department.

It is carried out, at some point, during a film's production or immediately after a film has wrapped when the artists still have the same 'look' as they did in the movie. The reason for a specials shoot is twofold:

1. Provide images for use in key artwork - posters and teaser posters

2. Prime editorial coverage

Miss Potter poster

This poster is a prime example of working in close harmony with a film distributor's marketing department, who provided me with clear concepts prior to the shoot, which were delivered and subsequently became the poster.

©Momentum Pictures - photo: Alex Bailey

KODAK EPP MAMIYA RZ **180MM** 1/250 **F16** STROBE

Angelina Jolie as Lara Croft in
Lara Croft Tomb Raider: The Cradle of Life

Specials shoots provide the images for key art which has
varying end uses, hence the need to provide different
images.

Lara Croft Tomb Raider: The Cradle of Life
©Courtesy of Paramount Pictures
Photo: Alex Bailey

Due to their financial independence, the marketing people can work to their own brief. They will have concepts, in the form of drawings, prepared by a design agency showing a suggested poster campaign. These will be presented to the film-makers and artists involved prior to the specials shoot, as their approval and cooperation is required.

These concepts will often draw on images already provided by the stills photographer along with other visual references depicting the aspirations of a marketing theme.

The specials shoot usually benefits from a dedicated day with the artists, either on location when a makeshift studio will be set up or in a proper photo studio if available.

It is very likely that sets, or part of sets, will be needed, as will various appropriate props from the film. The hair, make-up and costume departments will be called on for the specials shoot, which may conflict with their requirement to be on set if the film is shooting at the same time, so extra crew may be needed to cover for them. Collectively a lot to organize, overseen by the unit publicist.

The specials photographer, and staff are independent from the film production, organizing their own equipment and travel arrangements etc.

Due to the quality of the material required, the specials shoot will be shot high resolution on most likely medium format digital, with its excellent large screen play-back facility and the reassurance that it brings to the anxious marketing people and a representative from the design agency who also ensures that the correct coverage is achieved from the very important specials shoot.

I cannot honestly say I know why it is called a specials shoot, maybe it is because the photographers that are sometimes commissioned to shoot specials are 'special' themselves?

I have certainly worked on films where some of the top name photographers have been commissioned for the specials shoot: Annie Leibovitz, Herb Ritts, David LaChapelle, and Albert Watson, to name but a few.

I would not question the logic as to why they, instead of me, are sometimes asked to do the shoot. If only for the very fact that their images, based on who they are, will guarantee coverage in quality publications is reason enough.

I am quite philosophical as to whether I am asked to do the specials shoot or not, as I completely appreciate the various benefits an alternative photographer can bring to the range of photographical material representing a movie, not least another photographer's reputation and abilities.

On some movies I am simply too busy to do justice to an alternative photo shoot that would divide my loyalty with the on set photography. Arguably, it is easier to come onto a film for just a few days and shoot to 'get a job done' without having to get overly involved with the daily mechanics of a production.

At other times, when I am already the stills photographer on a film, and the pace is quite modest, I welcome the opportunity to do the specials shoot as well, with all the challenges and organization it will require.

KODAK EPP MAMIYA RZ **180MM** 1/250 **F16** STROBE

Angelina Jolie as Lara Croft in
Lara Croft Tomb Raider: The Cradle of Life

Variation on a theme.

Lara Croft Tomb Raider: The Cradle of Life
©Courtesy of Paramount Pictures
Photo: Alex Bailey

Bijou Phillips during filming of Octane

Specials shoots also provide images for magazines, the inspiration for the photos usually comes from the film, the look of the artist, props from the set etc. But the artist also expresses their own individual personality by maybe wearing their own clothes or the way they use props etc. A sort of halfway house. The photo illustration for an article or interview is then relevant, the film is represented so is the individual actor, the words can then cover both angles the character in the film and the actor as a person.

©Alex Bailey - photo: Alex Bailey
courtesy Random Harvest

KODAK EPP MAMIYA RZ **50MM**
1/250 **F8** STROBE

Leo Gregory, Bijou Phillips,
Mischa Barton
and Jonathan Rhys Meyers
during filming of Octane

Specials photography with particular
marketing concepts in mind.

©Alex Bailey - photo: Alex Bailey
courtesy Random Harvest

equipment and lighting as well as liaising
with the production, if sets are to be built
and props required. In order to do this
he will need the resources of at least two
other assistants, one to look after the
camera and its technical needs, as I now
shoot on medium format digital opposed
to film, and another lighting assistant,
sometimes more depending
on the size of the shoot and variation
of set-ups required.

I deal with the creative side: actors,
hair and make-up, costume, the lighting
and the style of photography.

On some productions, I have been
asked to run a specials studio adjacent
to filming, for weeks in order to
photograph the principal actors at
convenient times when they are not
needed for filming.

The first call I make, when commissioned
and presented with the concepts for a
specials shoot to contemplate, is to my
trusted number one assistant Simon.
He is the one I rely heavily upon to
organize, deliver and oversee the setting
up of most of the photographic

It is an expensive exercise when hired cameras, lighting, photo studios and assistants are involved. But paled into insignificance compared to the importance of producing images that the marketing and publicity campaign will be built on.

In these circumstances, I continue to cover the set during filming and dash off to the photo studio when an actor becomes available for stills. Due to the immediacy of the situation, I will need to walk into the studio in operating mode, hence the need for an attentive professional team to back me up.

The success of a specials shoot depends largely on the preparations prior to it taking place. The various concepts proposed by the design agency will require at least a day or two setting up, allowing time to build sets and backdrops, to perfect lighting with stand-ins and gather component parts such as props or costumes.

Time with the actors is precious and is best spent achieving the required images rather than ironing out technicalities. So everything equipment wise must be well tried and tested before the event.

Adaptability and the need to work quickly is an advantage due to the eclectic nature of a specials shoot, which have a habit of veering off in different 'creative' directions. This can often be due to an actor's welcomed input and interpretation of what is required from the concepts, that act as only a guideline to the content of the photos and are seldom strictly adhered to.

Angelina Jolie as Lara Croft in
Lara Croft Tomb Raider: The Cradle of Life

From one of the several shoots on Tomb Raider, with Angelina Jolie producing excellent generic marketing images.

Lara Croft Tomb Raider: The Cradle of Life
©Courtesy of Paramount Pictures
Photo: Alex Bailey

KODAK EPP MAMIYA RZ 110MM 1/250 F16 STROBE

Cliff Curtis, Michelle Yeoh, Cillian Murphy and Troy Garity in Sunshine

We built a light wall with nine 3200j flash heads in soft boxes shooting through a 20m square silk hung on an 'H' frame, to get the effect of the cast walking out of a light tunnel.

HASSELBLAD HD DIGITAL 100ISO **100MM** 1/500 **F11**

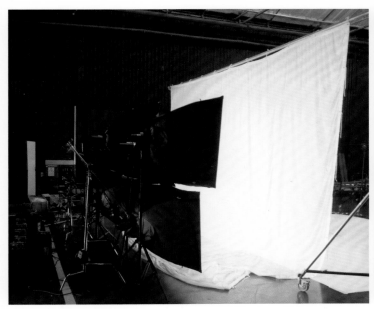

Lighting rig for light wall.

©imagebarn - photo: Alex Bailey

Whilst the photography that is produced on set by the stills photographer constitutes a substantial part of the images used for the marketing (possibly even the poster), and in particular the publicity for a movie, it is often the images from a specials shoot that the marketing campaign will revolve around. Hence their importance and consequently the pressure felt by those in the marketing departments that instigate the shoot. Once the shoot is over and the images are in the can, or nowadays on the hard drive, the relief for all those concerned is palpable.

All that remains is for the clever people at the design agency to develop the images into stunning posters in an attempt to entice the public to see the movie when it is released. The pressure is on again!

From my experience, it is about a fifty-fifty split between images from the film set via the stills photographer and those from a specials shoot that become the key art or poster for a film, a combination of both is not unusual.

Whatever happens, photos from specials shoots almost certainly get used as covers and spreads in magazines. Often offered to publications on an exclusive basis.

DIGITAL RAW FILE 800ISO **135MM** 1/200 **F3.5** 5300K

A perspective shot that I saw on a location in
East London. Railway bridges are boring but
necessary. Like financial issues.

The Business of Business

There is no doubt, an understanding of financial matters is a contributing factor to an individual's potential success.

In real terms, this means charging for ones services at a realistic level and maintaining control over your cash flow, not ignoring the issues of bills and tax.

I know this sounds dull, but I am afraid it is a fact of life, no matter how creative you are, you will simply not survive if you do not deal competently with the mundane matters relating to money and its management.

The world is full of 'artistic' people that did not fulfil their potential because they could not manage their finances.

The constituent parts of photography coupled with the advent of digital capture requires the purchasing of expensive equipment, which in turn requires careful thought and consideration. I would recommend to any aspiring photographers that they should take advice from trusted mentors, be that fellow professionals, an accountant or employer as to the financing, and type of equipment to purchase which, when operating at a professional level will need regular maintenance and renewal.

Up to date, very reliable tools are a prerequisite for the job.

As equally important as managing money matters is how one conducts oneself professionally. A potential client's first contact is usually either by email or on the telephone.

First impressions count for everything; a professional prompt response to any enquiry for your services is always well received and starts you off in the right direction, maintained by keeping in regular contact with your clients.

The excellent representation of your work is also very important. Employers often consider the presentation of an individual's work as a barometer to their professional conduct. If a portfolio is disorganised, chances are so will the owner be.

DIGITAL RAW FILE 800ISO 100MM 1/160 F2.8 5300K

Atonement

I always look out for poignant props on a set, on the dower subject of finances I thought this appropriate.

Atonement James McAvoy

KODAK EPP RATED @ 50ISO **X PROCESSED** 20MM **1/125** F5.6

This photo has a surreal feel enhanced by cross processing, full frame of course.

Even if the content is good, an employer will still question the individual's ability to conform with their routine. As a stills photographer, in the film business, you have the responsibility of managing a substantial budget, plus the need to respectfully conduct oneself in the company of a broad cross section of colleagues. A sloppy or unregimented presentation of ones portfolio does tend to infer a lackadaisical attitude to a structured environment, which a film most definitely is.

A film can be likened to an army with the higher-ranking officers, the majors, colonels and lieutenants being your producers, directors and HODs with their second in commands being the sergeants and corporals down to the general crew - the privates.

A film production, like an army, needs to have a degree of discipline and respect in order to function efficiently. So I would not suggest: 'Yes sir, no sir, three bags full sir'. But I would suggest a polite amiable and efficient attitude when dealing with any rank.

Certainly professional conduct is important, as is good business management, which can make or break a creative career.

But ultimately it is the determination and desire to succeed that must go hand in hand with a knowledgeable and motivated approach to photography that will consolidate a career producing marketing and publicity images for the film and TV industry.

Nonso Anozie and Daniel Mays
in Atonement

An evocative image of soldiers walking through a poppy field, I love the sense of movement from their legs in the poppy stems, like wading through waves. A slight diagonal adds to the feeling of movement and the sun's position is perfect for my taste.

DIGITAL RAW FILE 250ISO **25MM** 1/60 **F7.1** 5500K

Credits

Stills Photography

The Boat That Rocked

RocknRolla

The Other Boleyn Girl

Atonement

Miss Potter

Sunshine

The History Boys

Mrs Henderson Presents

Pride and Prejudice

Troy

Phantom of the Opera

Lara Croft:Tomb Raider

Lara Croft Tomb Raider:The Cradle Of Life

Bridget Jones's Diary

Enemy at the Gates

The Four Feathers

Elizabeth

Thunderpants

An Ideal Husband

Some Voices

Pandemonium

Still Crazy

Sliding Doors

Spiceworld The Movie

The Borrowers

Richard III

Angels & Insects

Twelfth Night

Funny Bones

Specials

Miss Potter

Mission: Impossible III

Sunshine

Mrs Henderson Presents

The Descent

Lara Croft:Tomb Raider

Lara Croft Tomb Raider:The Cradle Of Life

Lassie

Thunderpants

Enemy at the Gates

King Lear

Auf Wiedersehen Pet

The Music of Andrew Lloyd Webber

Complicity

An Ideal Husband

Pandaemonium

Some Voices

Still Crazy

The Borrowers

The Clandestine Marriage

Sliding Doors

The Madness of King George

Keep The Aspidistra Flying

Glossary of Film Terms
used in Movie Photos

ANAMORPHIC extra wide panoramic ratio 2.39:1 opposed to 35mm 1.37:1

ANORAK a waterproof coat, colloquial term for a geek or a nerd

APERTURE lens opening measured in stops, works based on halving or doubling the light exposed to the film plane, associated with depth of field

APPROVALS the process of acquiring consent to use an image

ASSISTANT DIRECTORS
1ST AD runs the floor
2ND AD runs the artists
3RD AD liaises between 1st and 2nd

ART anything created by man requiring thought

ATMOS short for atmosphere - refers to smoke or haze on set

BABY LEGS small tripod

BACKLOT exterior shooting area of a film studio where outdoor sets are built

BLIMP soundproof housing for a camera

BLOCKING THROUGH the process of planning a scene for technical analysis

BLUE OR GREEN SCREEN backdrop used when shooting effects or CGI shots

BOOM extending pole used by a sound person with a microphone and cable attached

BOOM OP person that holds the boom

CABLE BASHER person that carries a cable, sound, camera etc.

CALL SHEET the daily issued itemized list of who, what and where happens on the set

CGI computer generated images

CHECKING THE GATE the gate is where the film is exposed in a movie camera, checking it ensures nothing has encroached in this area which could result in scratches on the film's emulsion or reproduce as a blob or line. 'Hair in the gate', has become check the chip for digital.

CHERRY PICKER crane usually for mounting a light on

CHIP SHOP carpenters work shop

CIRCLES OF CONFUSION relates to the acceptable sharpness of an image at viewing distance

CLAPPER LOADER the person that loads the movie film into the magazine (or replaces the drive in digital) and claps the board at the beginning and end of a take for the benefit of synchronizing the sound

CLOSED SET restricted access to a set

CONTINUITY the ensuring of correct details between takes

COLOUR TEMPERATURE the colour content of light measured in degrees kelvin

CUTAWAYS insert shots

CUTTING ROOM where movie editing is carried out

DEPTH OF FIELD the distance between two acceptably sharp points of focus

DEPTH OF FOCUS the distance along a lens axis through which the film may be moved before the image at a point on the subject becomes noticeably unsharp.

DGA Directors Guild of America

DIFFUSERS collective term for anything, that dilutes a light source

DIRECTOR the person that directs a movie

DISTRIBUTORS the company responsible for releasing a film theatrically

DOLLY piece of equipment the movie camera is mounted on when tracking

DOP Director of photography, the person that decides the lighting and lens

DUTCH off centre camera angle

EFX an effects shot

EPK Electronic press kit. A visual press kit made for television and radio to promote the film's release. Includes interviews with key cast and crew, behind the scenes footage, 'the making of', and clips from the finished film.

EYELINE direct view of a person

EXTRAS supporting artists required to fill a scene as crowd, background etc

FILL IN relates to putting light in a dark area

FLAG piece of equipment used for masking spill light

FLOOR RUNNER junior assistant director

GEL light transmitting coloured sheet put over a light

GIRAFFE type of crane used to mount the movie camera on

GO AGAIN repeat of the last take

GRADING technical adjustments made to the footage at the lab by the DOP

HAIR IN THE GATE an obstruction in the movie camera's gate, (point of

exposure) likely to cause scratching or an unwanted image on the film

HAPPY SNAPS photos for cast and crew not required for publicity and marketing purposes

HERO when used in the context of a film relates to the importance of an individual item

HONEY WAGON the crew's location toilet

HOD head of department

JIBBING the act of raising the movie camera on the dolly during a take

KEY ART poster - or main images for a films promotion

KILLS images deleted by a person with approval of their likeness

LIPSTICK CAMERA very small worm like camera

LUMENS measure of brightness or brilliance

LOW-LOADER a lorry with a low floor and no sides

MARKS points of reference for sharps put down by a focus puller

MONITORS playback video screens

MOVEMENT ORDER detailed directions to a location

NETTING soft focus on lens by means of a stocking

NEUTRAL DENSITY FILTER filter with no colour bias that restricts light in increments normally stops and half stops

NIGHT SHOOT filming during darkness hours, during the night

NOISE BOYS collective name for the sound department

OFF CAMERA out of shot - not scene by the camera

PAN left to right movement of a camera

PANAGLASS eye protector comes in different densities used for looking at bright light source, the sun, large filming lights without damaging eye.

PER DIEM allowance given to cast and crew when on location

PHOTOGRAPH two dimensional representation of a three dimensional object

PHOTO OPS' photo opportunities

POLARIZING FILTER filters certain wavelengths of reflected light. Useful for increasing saturation, reducing reflections from polished surfaces and controlling highlights

POST-PRODUCTION the stage after the film has been shot, when it is edited, the soundtrack laid down and all elements completed before delivery to the distributors/sales agents

PRE-PRODUCTION the period before a film starts shooting when all the production preparations are made

PRESS RELEASE statement issued to the press giving approved information on a product or event, normally written by the relevant publicist

PRODUCER the person responsible for putting together film projects and overseeing them during production

PRODUCTION NOTES written by the unit publicist they tell the story behind the film, include any historical information and main cast and crew biographies

PROPS items on a set

PUBLICIST person responsible for a movie's publicity requirements during production

PYROTECHNICS collective name for things that explode, smoke or burn for effect on set

REHEARSAL the chance for cast and crew to perfect their performance before a take

RESOLUTION fineness of detail

RUSHES film, stills or sound footage

SALES AGENTS a company that sells a movie to worldwide territories where there is not a distributor attached

SAG Screen Actors Guild, the nation's largest labour union representing working actors

SAUSAGE type of focus mark placed on the floor looks like a sausage, often coloured for a specific artist so they know which is their own mark

SCHEDULE break down of scenes and the days they will be filmed, including cast required

SCRIPT the words

SET DRESSING collective name for individual items or props on a set

SHARPS focus for the movie camera

SHOT LIST list of shots.

SILKS daylight diffusers

SFX special effects

SOUND STAGE soundproof stage for filming that sets are constructed on

SPLIT DAY half a day shoot and half a night shoot together

STANDBYS carpenters, painters. plasterers, riggers for example who are on set during filming in case their services are required.

STAND IN person who stands in for an actor while the technicalities are sorted out

STEADICAM mobile camera rig attached to a camera operator

STICKS another name for a standard tripod

STORYBOARD hand drawn visualization of a scene shot by shot

STRIKE de-rig, break-up or deconstruct a film set

SQUIB effects bullet hit

SWING A LENS change lenses

TAKE committing to film or hard drive

TILT up and down movement of a camera

TRACE type of diffusing material, essentially tracing paper in varying thicknesses

TRACKING a moving shot

TRACK the rails the dolly sits on for a tracking shot

TREATMENT appraisal of a script

TURN AROUND time between call times

TURNING OVER expression used when camera is running

TURNING AROUND reversing camera angle which involves reorganization of camera etc. on set

VIDEO VILLAGE the area designated to the playback monitors

VIEWING REHEARSAL a technical rehearsal of a scene

WEATHER COVER alternative filming if the scheduled work is affected by adverse weather

WIRE WORK stunt work that requires wires being attached to an artist

WINNEBAGO mobile sleeping quarters for artists

WRAP end of filming

Jena Malone, Rosamund Pike,
Carey Mulligan, Talulah Riley,
Keira Knightley and Brenda Blethyn
in Pride and Prejudice

The ladies in Pride and Prejudice
enjoying a break in filming.

© 2005 Focus Features - photo: Alex Bailey
Courtesy of Universal Studios Licensing LLLP

KODAK PORTRA 500ISO **105MM** 1/125 **F5**

Back cover shot
Keira Knightley in Pride and Prejudice

© 2005 Focus Features - photo: Alex Bailey
Courtesy of Universal Studios Licensing LLLP

KODAK PORTRA 640ISO **180MM** 1/125 **F4**